The Gift of a Day

JEFF GLASBRENNER

ISBN: 1479131164
ISBN-13: 9781479131167

Library of Congress Control Number: 2012915012
CreateSpace Independent Publishing Platform, North Charleston, SC

ACKNOWLEDGEMENTS

I would like to thank my family and friends from the bottom of my heart. This journey has been so fun and meaningful because of your love and support. I would like to especially thank my children for inspiring me every day to continue to look at each day as a true gift!

CONTENTS

INTRODUCTION

Most people can pinpoint several significant days in their lives that made a difference in who and where they are. Typically people will give you their wedding day, the birth of a child, graduating from college, the death of a family member, etc... My days are actually somewhat different.

Don't get me wrong, my wedding day, the birth of my children, and college graduation have all been very meaningful in my life, but if you really think about it, those days are results of other days and choices you made before them. Each day you are presented with a "gift"—but do you always view it as a gift? That is your choice. It's easy to say the birth of your child was a gift, but it's not so easy to say that losing your leg was a gift.

This book will outline twelve days in my life that were truly gifts. Being an athlete, I have trained myself to have mental pictures of success. I trained my mind to think positively, and more times than not, positive things happen for me. When you get ready to face your day in front of you, do you view yourself at the top or just getting by?

I am an athlete. My wife tells me I am engaging and have a contagious smile. I am a husband and a father of two wonderful, beautiful children. I am passionate about sports and unwavering in my desire to share that passion with others. I am also a below-the-knee amputee who suffered the loss of my leg in a traumatic accident as an eight-year-old boy.

While the accident claimed my right leg, it couldn't take away my heart. Thirty-something years after that accident, I can boast an exceptional list of accomplishments: Wheelchair Basketball World Champion, Paralympic Games Bronze Medalist, and winner of multiple Ironman competitions competing as a physically challenged athlete, and I am still pressing on. Signifying my accident's thirtieth anniversary at the age of eight, I challenged myself to complete eight Ironman distance competitions within an eight month period (8-in-8). I believe that with hard work and a positive attitude, anyone can do anything—disability or not. If you think about it, we all have some sort of disability—mine just happens to be a sanctioned one. Are you overweight? Are you not muscular? Are you tired all the time? Are you a procrastinator? Does your back hurt? Do you work too much? Do any of these sound familiar? I could go on—these are all "disabilities" for each of us.

In my journey to meet that eight-Ironman-challenge, Ironman Wisconsin was on the list. This Ironman was particularly momentous given that, while I was competing, I ran past the hospital where I spent months recuperating as a child, where doctors told him me I would never be able to participate in sports again. I saw this race not only as the next challenge in my quest, but a chance to witness my life coming full circle.

I created "Team G.L.A.S."—a motivational speaking business designed to teach others how to Grow, Live, Accomplish, and Succeed. Taking the lessons I've learned in life and in sports, I've used my speaking engagements and competitions as living examples of how to overcome obstacles.

People often look at me and say that I make it look easy. I've suffered many painful days to reach my moments of victory. The difference between me and others who've suffered is that I view those painful days—physical and emotional—as fuel to get me to victory. Victory can be defined in many ways. It's not just crossing a finish line or winning a game. Victory can be as simple as smiling at your children's laughter, getting up in the morning to work out, or feeling tired at the end of the day, but feeling you lived your day to the fullest.

This book is written to remind you each day that you have a choice. Take the gifts that are given to you **every** day of your life. Learn to recognize them as gifts and take them as your own.

DAY 1: LOSING MY LEG

"To have become a deeper man
is the privilege of those who have suffered."
–Oscar Wilde

I was born and raised in a small farming community in the southwest corner of Wisconsin. My family of seven was tight-knit. We had to be—we shared one bathroom for the entire family in our cozy farmhouse.

I am the oldest of five children. I grew up with a strong emphasis on work ethic. Each of my siblings and I had chores, responsibilities, and duties on the farm. My family owned a registered, polled Hereford cow farm, and it was a year-round job for all of us.

All the Glasbrenner kids would help with the crops in the summer and then transition to caring for the animals in the winter. During the summer months, the cows were allowed to graze at their leisure in the pastures, and it was time to grow and harvest the hay crop their land produced. When the Wisconsin winter turned brutally cold, the animals would be fed and sheltered in the barns.

Although hard work was valued, we were also allowed some fun. I loved to swim at the pool in town, five miles away. My siblings and I would go there for special occasions during the summer. Running was also a love. I not only loved it, I was good at it. I won all the races against the other schoolboys. My family always encouraged my athletics and they recognized my talent very early. My dad was especially proud of my tenacity in sports.

Like most young boys, I was a shadow of my father. Whatever my dad set out to do, I was determined to do it with him and to learn from him. Growing up, I idolized my father. Jeffrey Carroll Glasbrenner was a hard worker and he expected a lot from his oldest son. He wasn't always nice about it or emotionally encouraging—there just wasn't any other option. You worked hard and you didn't stop until it was done correctly. Clearly this work ethic has resonated in me.

The morning of July thirtieth was hot and clear—perfect weather for harvesting. My dad and I filled the tractor with gas and got the mower ready for the day ahead. My Mom yelled her usual, "You two be careful," to which we always replied, "Ok Mom! See you later." There was nothing unusual or different about this day.

We got to work in the hayfield and starting cutting. After a few rounds in the field, the tractor made an abrasive, but familiar sound when the blade collided with a rock. It happened all the time due to the rocky soil of the southwestern Wisconsin fields—this was the main reason farm kids accompanied their parents on the tractor, to jump off and help remove obstacles in the tractor's way. The work went so much faster with me, a kid, present to do the "dirty work."

When the blade hit a rock, my dad habitually turned off the power-takeoff. We had this routine down to an art, plus I was getting that time with my dad that I wanted. After the machine was off, I would get off my "safe spot" on the tractor where I perched, waiting to be of use. I then walked around the mower, removed all the excess alfalfa and pulled out the rock that was causing the problem. Normally, I would get back on my perch, my father would turn the equipment back on, and we would continue cutting. We had done this hundreds of times.

This morning was the same as every other day. When he heard the tractor blade scrape against the rock, Dad turned off the tractor. It was my time to help, so I quickly got off my safe spot and went to work completing my job. I successfully removed the rock and went back around the mower to get back onto the safe spot, but before I got there, my dad turned on the machine.

In a split second, my life changed forever. The power-take-off on the back of the tractor caught my right pant leg. Before either of us knew what happened, I was thrust from the left hand side of the tractor to the right. The power-takeoff was powerful and unforgiving, and I became a victim of the whirling blades. My little leg was as helpless as a pencil in a pencil sharpener.

People often ask me if I remember the accident. I tell them, *like it was yesterday.* Lying on the ground in shock, I remember looking down to find only bone sticking out where there used to be a shin, an ankle, a foot, and healthy skin. Blood was gushing out uncontrollably, and the skin that was left had been ripped to shreds. I looked to my right and ten feet away was my shoe with a foot still in it.

Dad turned off the power-takeoff and in a rush scooped up my maimed body. Thankfully, he then had the presence of mind to apply a human hand tourniquet. He leaned over me and wrapped his hands as tightly as he could around my leg, just above the wound to try and minimize the bleeding. Doctors later told us that is what saved my life.

I began to sob, but not out of pain. My body was in too much shock to even register what had just occurred. I shed tears of fear. *What was my life going to be like? How was I going to walk?* I saw my future as a one-legged person flash before my eyes. No more running. No more playing. No more swimming. No more riding a bike. No more anything as I had innocently expected it to be. I was eight-years-old, and all I could think about was what I wasn't going to be able to do.

My dad—realizing the magnitude of what happened—was worried there wouldn't be a tomorrow for me. As if he could read my mind, he looked me in the eyes and said, "Son, let's get through today, and we will worry about the rest of the stuff later." Those words have stuck with me.

The neighbor's house was closer than going all the way back home, so my dad rushed me there. The neighbors had a car renowned for never starting, but that day the engine revved and we sped to the hospital with me bleeding all over the back seat. My mom got wind of the accident from her sister up the road. On her trip to the hospital, she didn't know which Jeff had been injured—her husband or her son.

They rushed me to the local hospital in Boscobel, Wisconsin. Boscobel—a small farming community—hardly had the appropriate medical care for an injury of this magnitude. All they could do was pack my leg with ice, transfuse blood into my body to replace the huge amount I had lost, and send us on a seventy-mile ambulance ride bound for the University of Wisconsin Hospital in Madison. There was no medical evacuation helicopter available.

During the initial journey in the ambulance, I was awake. I remember wanting to look out the window, because the drive to Madison was one of my favorite car rides as a child. The scenery was beautiful and I wanted to see it again, but the attendants restrained me and told me to lie down and be still. Every time I moved, the blood flow increased to the leg and caused blood to gush from the split arteries.

For the rest of the ride, I was in and out of consciousness. All I remember after that was feeling frustrated with the emergency team asking me the same questions over and over again. Mom was in the ambulance with me, but Dad was not. The doctors had sent him on a mission to retrieve my severed limb in case, by some miracle, they were able to use it. He went back to the field to look for the shoe with my foot in it. After an hour or so, my father returned to the hospital with my shoe – foot and all. The doctors were unable to use the severed limb. However,

I was told later that some of my skin from my foot was able to be used on a burn patient that was also in the hospital.

When they rushed me into the Madison hospital, they told my Mom she could not enter the Emergency Room where they were about to perform a series of medical procedures to try and save my life, but she forced her way in the door and did not leave my side.

Once at the hospital I spent the next forty-seven days fighting for my life. The farming equipment in the accident was so dirty it had contaminated the wound and exposed flesh on my leg. I contracted gangrene, and infection quickly took hold of my body.

The blood loss, compounded by the increasing gangrene infection, caused my heart to stop beating. Doctors were forced to jump start my heart on two different occasions. I underwent thirteen different operations to rid my body of infection and try and save as much of my leg as possible. In 1980, medical treatments weren't what they are today. They grafted skin from different places on my back and buttocks to save as much of the leg as they could.

Doctors advised my family to let them remove the knee to keep the gangrene from spreading up the leg any further, but my Dad fought them and insisted they try to keep my knee. I, to this day, don't know how he knew to insist on that for my quality of life, but his insistence that the knee be preserved—although it seemed risky at the time—enables me to do what I do today.

On several occasions, I had to go into surgeries back to back, so I was forced to fast sometimes for twenty-four hours.

I remember crying from being frustrated, hungry, and in pain from wounds and needle poking. Those forty-seven days of hospital life took their toll on my entire family, including me.

One of the few things that kept me going during these traumatic forty-seven days were my friends and family. They brought me Star Wars action figures, spaceships, and posters. My room at the end of my stay looked more like the galaxy than a hospital room. People were always coming to visit, and my family made sure I had someone there at all times.

The nurses also warmed up to me. They would let me have syringes so I could use them as miniature water guns and squirt my guests as they walked in the door. It was one of the few comic reliefs they could offer. Little did I know, I would teach my own children that trick in the hospital during their illnesses.

The recovery after the hospital wasn't easy. I knew my whole life was different, and at first I didn't embrace it. I was on crutches for months as my prosthetic leg was being formed, and I spent most of my days sitting on the couch flipping through both stations we had on our TV. The "Duke" boys became my outlet.

A few months after my accident, I was at the table eating dinner and excused myself to use the restroom. I got up, took a first step, and fell flat on my face. Like many amputee victims of traumatic accidents, I still to this day have most of the nerve endings in place, meaning I have the sensation of my whole leg being attached. In my mind, I can still wiggle my toes and rotate my ankle.

When I took that first step thinking my leg was intact—only to be reminded abruptly of its absence—I hit rock bottom, emotionally. Lying on the kitchen floor, I covered my face with my hands in embarrassment and frustration and I began to cry. I remember just wanting this whole experience to go away. I didn't like being different, disabled, or an amputee. I desperately wanted to be normal again. I wanted my leg back.

Like any eight-year-old, I was extremely challenged to cope with my new existence as an amputee. I wasn't capable of thinking positively yet. Thoughts like, "Now I only have to tie one shoe," or, "For Halloween this year, I can be a pirate with a real wooden leg," weren't where I focused my mental energy.

I was dwelling on the opposite—all the things in life I would never be able to do and all of the opportunities I now had to give up. I quickly fell into the trap of letting everyone do everything for me, from getting a Coke, to opening a door, to putting on my clothes. In short, after coming home from the hospital, I settled into a deep depression and became very dependent on the couch and my family.

DAY 2: COKE

"Adversity is the first path to truth."
–Lord Byron

Before the accident, I enjoyed the invaluable innocence of child-hood. I was happy and fun loving, tried anything, and always sought out adventure. After the accident, I felt more like a damaged vessel. In my mind, I had been unexpectedly anchored out to sea. Hopeless, I began to accept my static existence.

The seas I traversed were no longer the backyard, the playgrounds, the swimming pool, and the hay fields. I now sunk, stagnant, on the couch, no longer wanting or thinking I could have that adventure. I was eight and my innocence had disappeared.

For months, my family centered on me, being careful not to insult or injure me in my fragile state. They bent over backward to make sure I was always comfortable, to ensure I was never stressed, and to cater to my every need. I, meanwhile, flipped through our two channels and waited for nothing and everything. Loneliness was my closest companion.

My mother had been standing by the whole time, arguably the most affected witness to my accident. She remembered the day of the accident and what had transpired like it was yesterday. She wrote me a letter a few years ago, recounting the incident and what we went through:

Letter from my mother:

We were on our way home from a short Door County vacation and decided we would stay overnight with your Great Aunt Marsh and Great Uncle Earl, and maybe visit some of our favorite Milwaukee sights. Your Grandma and Grandpa Glasbrenner were visiting with them when we arrived. We talked it over and your Dad said we really should just drive on home so he could cut some hay. We all slept in, probably still before 7:00 AM, but late for us. Your Dad asked you and your sister whose turn it was to go with him to help pull the hay off the mower when it plugged up. You decided it was your turn that day, so off you and your Father went, you riding safely—or so we thought—behind him on our John Deere 60. You both loved to spend time with your Dad. His first passion was farming, but it took your Dad working full time at John Deere & Company and me teaching full time to have enough money to farm. The field you were mowing was the long one up by the "Hippie Farm" across from our farm's spring. Some new neighbors had moved in and we really didn't know them real well.

The green beans in the garden were ready to be picked and canned, so I set off for the garden, giving Jenelle the job of watching your baby brother while I picked beans. I hadn't picked many beans when I heard the sound of the neighbor's car coming down the road. I remember looking up and thinking the fool didn't even stop at the stop sign. Normally, his car didn't run well enough to go that fast! I went back to my bean picking and then I heard Aunt Kathy's voice and could see her running down the road screaming, "One of the Jeffs have been hurt! You need to get to the hospital as fast as you can!" Aunt Kathy took Jenelle and Justin to her house—even though she runs a beauty shop there at her home—and I took off for the Boscobel Hospital, which was only five miles away, but it seemed like it took forever to get there. I remember praying all the way, **Let it be husband Jeff and NOT my little boy.** *My husband would be older and stronger to handle the accident. I remember praying,* **Please God let it just be a broken leg, please!**

When I arrived at the hospital the nurses told me it was my son. My worst nightmare. They told me I couldn't go in and I remember telling them in no uncertain words that was my little boy in there and I was going in. Well, I totally wasn't prepared for what I was about to see—there was my little eight-year-old Jeffrey lying on the table with his leg gone! I passed completely out! The doctors and nurses now had two problems. I came around pretty fast and told them I would be all right and would be going back in to be with my son who needed me! I learned at that time that your father had applied a tourniquet back in the field and they were in the process of changing that so they could move him to the University of Wisconsin Hospital in Madison.

When the Boscobel Rescue Squad arrived I was relieved to see your Uncle Tim Brown was one of the EMTs. He was the one responsible for keeping your foot and leg on ice. They let me ride with you in the ambulance and to me it seemed like it took forever. Every time they would put the siren on you would try to sit up and would say, "I just want to look out the window." You even asked why the cars were pulling off to the side of the road. The nurses were so good about explaining to you what was going on. They expected you to go into shock, but you never did. We arrived at the hospital in less than an hour; pretty good considering it was about eighty-five miles from Boscobel. The hospital personnel kept me busy with forms while they prepared you for surgery, the first of about fourteen. They put you in the Intensive Care Unit after that first surgery and you stayed there about ten days. The hardest part of those first few days was that they kept waking you up to tell you that you had lost your leg and then they would ask you if you remembered what happened. You would cry out "Mom, where is my Mom?" It was so hard to see you suffering so much. I thought that was so cruel to not only you, but to all of us. They reassured me that if they didn't there was a big chance you would/could go into shock. They called Code Blue for you at least three times. It was so hard to see them all come rushing in to take care of you! They were all so compassionate and professional.

You were in the University Of Wisconsin Hospital for the next forty-seven days. They were long and stressful, but we still had you! You had about fourteen different surgeries. Each time they would have to debride the wound, each time they would take a little more off. They repeatedly told us they had to have at least eight inches of stump in order for you to use a below-the-knee prosthesis, which would be the best route to go. Each night before surgeries, the doctors would always have me sign papers that showed that I accepted the risk you might die and that told me what we were in for as far as recovery. Your Grandpa Wilcox came down to see you about every other day and would bring some kids to try and cheer you up, and of course Grandpa would bring something for you even if was just French fries and a hamburger from McDonalds.

Many times, because of the nature of your wound, they would do you last and at least two times they let you go all day without eating or drinking and then show up and say they didn't have time and you would be scheduled for the surgery sometime tomorrow. I was never real assertive before this happened to you but it only took two times for me to say **enough.** I remember after the second time it happened taking the doctors out in the hall and saying, actually screaming, "How dare you put him through this? Do it to an adult they may understand, but never do it to my child again!" They apologized and reassured me it would never happen again, and it didn't.

The doctors were good but it was truly the nurses who saved your life and helped you deal with things medically and emotionally. The social workers at first were very concerned with all of us as a family group. They talked to us as a family and individually and decided we would be fine without counseling.

We met many wonderful people at that hospital. The children's floor was so wonderful and the nurses were so loving and caring. When your aunts and uncles—many were your age and younger—and your many cousins came to visit, you pretty much had the run of the floor. You were always such a cute little blonde with what the nurses said had the best manners, and you were always so appreciative which just made it easier for them to let you do whatever you and your little visitors wanted to do! The nurses even let you fill syringes with water and use them as *squirt guns! Many times the nurses would come out of your room soaked. The nurses thought you looked like John Schneider from the Dukes of Hazard, and so they often brought people down to see you. Most of the time they agreed!*

You had many special nurses, but I especially liked Heidi and Peter. Many days they would have to try four or five times to get an IV into your little body. The usual place was your arm, but toward the end of your stay they were putting them in your heel and foot—it usually took three or four nurses plus me to hold you down when they put them in.

One of the major surgeries you had was when they took skin off your back to graft onto your stump, and then took skin off your butt to put on your back. They put you in the burn center for this, because everything had to be sterile in order for it to take. They rotated you on a special bed and you hated the whole procedure. Many of the patients in this area had so much pain they would scream, and then you would scream, and I would just cry for you. You couldn't even go to the hospital's school and recreation area during this time, and your immediate family was the only type of visitors allowed.

You were always so sensitive about things. Whenever you would see me cry, you would cry and want to know what was wrong— so I had to be very careful about my own feelings, which at times was so hard! There was a boy from the Green Bay area that was dying of cancer and you thought you had cancer, because your room was next to his. His mother was one of the strongest people I ever had the opportunity to know. She gave me a piece of advice that I took to heart and used in raising you. "Many times a child with special needs' worst enemy is his mother, because she will either raise him to be independent or raise him to need everyone around him for the rest of his life." Jeffrey, you definitely are independent and have determination and drive beyond belief!

I am so sorry you went through this, but I am so proud of the man you have become.

Love, Mom

One memorable day my mom brought me a Coke in her hand, like usual, but as she handed it to me, she delivered an unexpected message. She promptly told me in her most stern voice, "This is the last Coke I will bring to you."

Surprised, I flippantly responded, "Can't you just go to town and pick up some more?"

Seeing that I clearly didn't understand her meaning, she tried again. "Oh, there are plenty of Cokes in the refrigerator, but that is the last Coke I am going to bring to you. From now on, you will be getting your own Cokes and everything else for that matter. You are no different than your brothers and sisters or anyone else, except for your negative attitude. And that's about to change."

Stunned, I was speechless. The person who had accommodated my needs for the past few months seemed to have abandoned me. How could she do this? Mom left the room and I was forced to think about her words.

At first, I felt sorry for myself, like many would. It was a hard message to absorb. I had grown accustomed to the path of least resistance, and what my mother was asking me to do now required every ounce of strength I had, but slowly I was coming around—I had to.

The first step was simply getting off the couch and going back to what *was* and now *would be again* my upstairs room. I started to get up and move around the house, no longer worried about opening doors, tripping, or the stares of my brothers and sisters. Before long, I was functioning like before—dressing myself, retrieving my own snacks and drinks, and even tagging along with my siblings to play or help out on the farm. I finally understood what my mother meant, and it was time to make some changes.

My mother has since told me how hard it was for her to do that to me. She would force me to do for myself and then go in the other room and worry with fear and cry. Thank God, though, for the mother of the child with cancer in the next room. She probably, emotionally, saved all of our lives with her words. Now that I am a father of a child with special needs, I am trying to impart that same wisdom to my children. It is a conscious effort every day to help our daughter reach her personal potential. And now, I fully understand just how hard it was for my Mom to let go and force me to fend for myself.

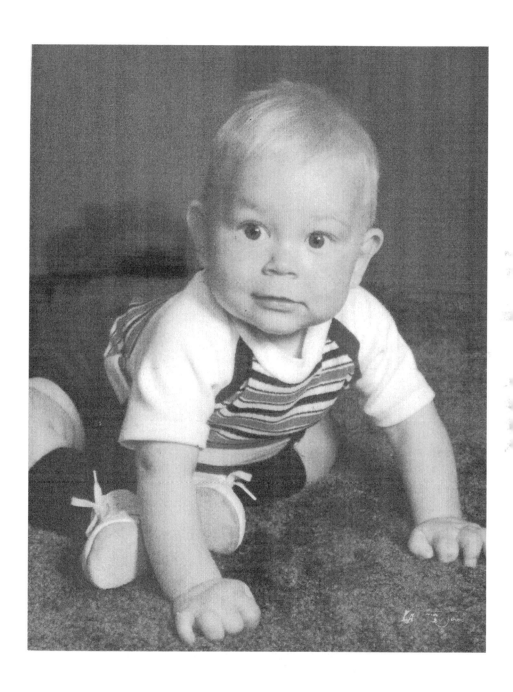

Above left: Always my dad's helper on the farm.
Above right: Discovering my love for John Deere tractors.

Below: Hanging out in the hospital with my relatives after losing my leg.

DAY 3: FIRST DAY OF WHEELCHAIR BASKETBALL

"Be not afraid of growing slowly;
be afraid only of standing still."
–Chinese Proverb

The first step was getting back to school. I returned to class that year in October and academically I was already six weeks behind the other kids. It was a new grade with new classmates and teachers, so all of my best buddies from the previous grade had been shuffled into other classes.

My family had decided to return me to school, even though I had not received my first prosthetic, which was still being molded. When my mom and I arrived in the school parking lot on my first day back, I looked out the car window and surveyed the scene before I touched the handle of the door. From the passenger seat window, I looked just like every other kid going into school—toting a backpack and lunch box. But as I stepped out of the car, it was just as I had imagined and feared it would be. Kids and parents glanced awkwardly in my direction, trying to hide their stares and curiosity. I heard the whispers as the children saw, not only the crutches, but that I had no right leg below the knee. It was torture.

In the classroom, I felt behind physically as well as scholastically. My teachers were understanding of the situation and did the best they could to make me feel at ease. The school itself was very accommodating. I was given one of those squares on wheels that you use to move furniture to go through the lunch line so I would not have to juggle carrying a lunch tray with my crutches, and my teachers worked with me patiently as I caught up academically to the rest of my classmates who'd started the school year in August.

By winter, I began to feel settled into a routine and felt like I was at least on board with the curriculum, and I finally received my first prosthetic leg. I had been looking forward to this day because I now had what I thought would help me fit in. My excitement quickly turned to disappointment to find the new leg caused ample discomfort. It strapped on—held together by Velcro, it was a waistband connected to a belt strap worn around the thigh that held the prosthetic onto the base of my knee.

I thought I would feel relief when the prosthetic arrived. I dreamed of how easy it would be to wear pants to cover up the missing leg. No one would stare anymore. I saw it as one step closer to feeling normal, but I was surprised to experience how foreign and uncomfortable the new prosthetic was. I couldn't make it part of me. It wasn't real. It didn't replace what I had lost or make it easier. Every time I put weight on the prosthetic to walk, it reminded me of how it didn't really belong. It hurt.

Since I really had no other options at the time, I functioned with the prosthetic while I was at school, and then took it off for relief at home where I would once again pick up the crutches.

That feeling of the prosthetic's "fakeness" never really diminished. One day, the kids in my class were playing kickball at recess and invited me to play. I loved sports so much, and being invited to play gave me a chance to feel a part of it all again. Maybe it wouldn't all be gone. My classmate rolled the big red kickball to me as I waited on home plate. I wound up and went for the kick and sent the ball soaring...followed by my prosthetic leg, which whirled through the air and landed with a thud on the ground. My face went white, and the kids broke out into laughter. Not knowing what else to do, I began to laugh along with them on the outside, but on the inside I was certain the doctors were right in their prediction—I would never play sports again.

Because I felt like sports were not an option for me, over the years, I decided I would have to find something else for me. I couldn't focus on my leg being gone forever. In school, I had never gravitated toward music or the arts, so in my mind I had very few choices. I ended up staying around sports, even though I felt like I couldn't play them. Often I was recruited to be the scorekeeper. I also discovered weight lifting in the school gym. It was the one place I could exercise and be a part of something the other kids did. I couldn't do any machines from the waist down, but I could work for hours on bicep curls and chest presses.

I also found enjoyment in showing my family's registered polled Herefords. I helped raise the cows from the time they were calves, and when it was time, I would show the cows for prize money. Many hours went into grooming and bathing the cattle before their shows. As a kid, I loved being out in the barn with the cattle and getting them loaded up for their big debut. Maybe it was the competition I really loved.

Transitioning into high school, I continued on as before. I always wore pants to help minimize the stares. I so desperately wanted my peers to see me as a person and not just a disability. Five years after wearing the strap-on prosthetic, I *finally* received a new leg with a cosmetic cover to make the faux leg look like it had real skin. The upgraded prosthetic added three pounds to my right leg and still felt like a burden.

As I went through high school, just like any boy I began to show interest in girls. My big and only real fear was that girls would let my disability get in the way of knowing the real me. I wasn't very aggressive about pursuing the dating scene. When I did date, I always wondered if they accepted me fully as I really was—disability included—but it gave me self-confidence as girls got to know me, and I made close friendships with the classmates who chose to know *the person,* not *the limitation.*

My siblings were very involved in sports, so I was often a spectator on the sidelines. I enjoyed watching my sister, Jenelle, play basketball, and would cheer for her and all of my friends who were on the court. She excelled and became one of the best players. I was very proud of her. I even did her chores for her at home while she stayed after school to practice. Her success was like my success. I lived through her. Her academics also seemed to come effortlessly. Jenelle was a straight-A student. I, on the other hand, did OK in class, but had to work to study and stay on top of my grades. As I grew older, I began to understand that I had the strongest work ethic, partly from having a dad who pushed me to never settle for less than I could achieve. As I watched my sister, I knew somewhere inside I was capable of doing the same thing, but that it would just take more effort on my part. It didn't make me bitter to watch—it made me realize how much I wanted to change my life to find my niche like she had so easily found hers.

When high school graduation came around, I didn't even contemplate college. I just wanted to take over the family farm and live at home. But again, Mom had other plans for me. She pushed me to go to college and said if I did want to farm, I needed an Agricultural Business degree. I remained living at home, but began attending class at the University of Wisconsin–Platteville.

After two years at Platteville, I realized I was ready to branch out and make a change. Jenelle attended the University of Wisconsin–Whitewater, where she was playing basketball. I was a typical college-aged boy ready to get out of the house, and decided I would go where my sister was. I ended up moving into the dorm at Whitewater, and that's where my life took a pivotal turn.

The new university had a larger campus, so I began to walk more than ever before. Back in my dorm room after the first week of class, I had taken off my prosthetic to give my leg some relief. During a study break, I decided to hop down to the bathroom instead of going through the trouble and pain of putting the prosthetic back on. On my way to the bathroom, a guy stopped me in my hobbling-path and said in an Australian accent, "Do you want to go play some basketball?" I gave him a funny look, as if to say, *Can't you see the obvious?* The guy raised up his pants to reveal he, too, was missing a limb. He went on to explain he was a member of Whitewater's wheelchair basketball team, something I had never heard of or thought of before. Wheelchair sports would never have dawned on me, because I wasn't in a wheelchair. My interest was piqued, and as I went back to his room, all of my past began to swarm through my head—all the doctor's warnings that I would never play sports, all the times I'd sat on the sidelines and watched someone else play. Could this be my chance to be an athlete? Could this be my gift?

My new acquaintance—who had come to the states to study and play on a collegiate team—brought me to the courts the next day, where I saw my first wheelchair basketball practice. The teammates maneuvered around the court with the ball as if the wheelchair was an extension of their bodies. I had never seen other people with disabilities do anything like this before. I had to give it a try.

The team members got me a wheelchair and invited me to try my hand at it. Of course, I wanted to be good at it right away. In fact, I *expected* to be a natural, based on how successful my sister had been at shooting hoops. The other guys made it look effortless and I mistakenly thought that meant it was easy. Remember this story the next time you see someone make something look effortless. In most cases, they worked tremendously hard to make it look that easy.

First of all, I had never used a wheelchair. Second, what little exposure to basketball I had mostly came from watching others and maybe shooting a few baskets in the driveway with my sister running circles around me. My first attempt to move the chair and coordinate ball travel was nearly impossible. Shooting from the seated position was completely different than standing, and I couldn't make a basket, or dribble and move, to save my life. Although discouraged, I knew I had found something significant—more than that—somewhere I felt like I *belonged* among others like me.

Then I met the wheelchair basketball team coach. The Coach watched me in my frustration trying to learn the new skills and shouted out, "How do you expect to be *great* never having done it before?"

After practice that day, Coach devised a plan for me. He challenged me—if I would show up every single morning at 5:30 a.m. to practice and develop the skills everyone else already had, Coach promised he would be there to meet me and help me catch up. He warned me though, "If you are late even once, our deal is off." For the next few months, I religiously came to the courts at 5:30 a.m. and practiced with Coach for an hour and a half before the rest of the team arrived.

Each and every day we practiced something new—a skill I needed to master to be able to play competitively on the team. Coach knew exactly what to show and teach me. He, too, was in a wheelchair having been paralyzed in a car accident at the age of eighteen. After playing for five years competitively, Coach decided to coach others and encourage those with disabilities.

Coach told me over and over again how much he enjoyed coaching me, because I was a "fresh egg" with no bad habits. I had come to wheelchair basketball with no vices, and Coach was able to download into my brain the correct and most efficient way to learn and play. I was a clean slate with one of the hardest work ethics Coach had ever seen. In addition to my solo practice in the early mornings and team practices each day, I was practicing extra on my own in the afternoons and evenings. Each day, I was putting in four to five hours of basketball on top of schoolwork.

Having never played adult sports prior to my first year at Whitewater, I had four full years of college athletic eligibility. I began traveling with the wheelchair basketball team once or twice a month to competitions. My hard work was starting to show in the games. I was scoring points and began to move on the court with ease and control.

Coach approached me alone one day and told me, "I believe you can make the national team, but you're going to have to work even harder than you do now. It's a new level of commitment. Do you want to try to make it?" Together, we developed a plan to make the national team a reality.

Before, I had trained four to five hours. Now, I practiced six to eight hours every day. I showed up to every practice with the mentality that if another player had more natural talent, I would make up the difference with hard work. I was talented as well as hard-working. After proving myself in numerous competitions, along with the recommendation from my coach, I received an invitation for the national team tryouts in 1997.

Tryouts were in Colorado Springs, and they consisted of a five-day training camp. One hundred wheelchair basketball athletes were invited to attend, but only the top twelve were selected to be on the current year's national team. For five days, I showed the coaches my work ethic, skills, and talent. I was chosen as one of the twelve.

1998 World Championship

In 1998, I went to compete at my first world championships in Australia. The small-town Wisconsin boy with a disability traveled out of the country for the first time to compete in a world championship event. It opened up a whole new world of experiences for me. The tournament lasted three weeks in Australia. My jump ball opponent from the Australian national team rolled up to meet me on the center court line—it was my friend from Whitewater, the college buddy who had stopped me in the dorm hallway to ask if I wanted to play basketball. My life, up until this point, had come full circle. I realized how far I had come and how thankful I was that I had been in the right place at the right time and had seized the opportunity. I recognized the gift being given to me and I took it gladly. I took the jump ball to start the game off with a punch, and as a twenty-five-year old athlete, I was a member of the American team that took home the world championship.

The World Championship was amazing. I got to share a room with David Kiley—a veteran player and mentor of mine. He took me under his wing and we formed a lasting friendship. We won our games pretty much at ease in pool plan. Our only real challenge was a game against Great Britain—we won fifty-six to fifty-one. The Gold medal game was against the Netherlands. The same Netherlands team we played earlier in the tournament where we won sixty-eight to fifty-two. It was their only loss in the tournament. This game, though, they had a different game plan. It was a game back and forth with our team leading at half time, thirty-three to twenty-eight. With one minute remaining, we were down, fifty-eight to fifty-nine. Then my teammate was fouled, making the shot and put in the extra point. We won in amazing fashion, sixty-one to fifty-nine. My first Gold Medal.

As an athlete, there is no greater feeling than wearing the USA uniform with a Gold medal around your neck while you listen to the National Anthem. I always strive for Gold medal moments in life. They are not always won on the court or in a sporting arena, but it can be anything in life for which you have a dream or goal, and you have the courage and conviction to work hard toward.

I hope all of you go for your own Gold medal moments in life.

DAY 4: MAKING THE PARALYMPIC TEAM

"Nothing can stop the man with the right mental attitude from achieving his goal;
nothing on earth can help the man with the wrong mental attitude."
–Thomas Jefferson

After winning the World Championships in 1998, I decided to stay in college and double major, since I had one more year of eligibility to play basketball. I had already obtained a marketing degree and decided to also major in Human Resources Management. Leading up to graduation that following year, I was playing basketball, but also thinking about the future in terms of finding a full-time career.

In the spring of 1999, my former teammate and roommate from the 1998 World Championship team, David, called me to talk about a job opportunity that had surfaced. David had attended a medical trade show and had crossed paths with someone interested in hiring me.

David had met a rep from a small medical sales company looking for a salesperson to focus on the wheelchair sports market. David had recently developed a signature wheelchair for basketball called the "David Kiley Quickie All Court Wheelchair." The owners of the company were interested in having me on board to help sell and promote the new chair.

My girlfriend at the time and I had both just graduated from the University of Wisconsin–Whitewater and I was all for relocating. The two of us decided to take a road trip to Winston-Salem, North Carolina for an official job interview. I wanted to get a closer look at the area and get more details on the job.

After scoping out the company and the central North Carolina area, we decided to make the move. I had talked this company into a decent salary and seven weeks of paid vacation so I could still travel to and train for all my wheelchair basketball events. I liked the company and the people I would be surrounded by. It seemed like a natural fit, given my experience and enthusiasm surrounding the product I would be representing.

Upon settling in a new apartment and beginning "real-life," I was given a few weeks of job training to familiarize myself with the wheelchairs and the other medical equipment I would be selling. On top of that, I also learned medical codes for the equipment and patient diagnoses. I shadowed another salesman to gain a better understanding of the day-to-day job. Soon thereafter, I was given my own territory and was set loose to start selling.

My newly assigned territory was not close to home, as I had been originally promised. I was spending at least two and a half hours each day in the car just to meet with clients. Although I enjoyed the customers and helping them find solutions and medical equipment, I didn't enjoy all the time behind the wheel, not to mention the paperwork.

Our company sold more Quickie All Court Wheelchairs that year than any other vendor in the United States. Another perk that came with my job was a sponsorship. Sunrise Medical— the maker of the wheelchair itself—offered me a sponsorship to personally use and endorse their product on the courts.

I was signed to play basketball with the Arkansas Rolling Razorbacks. That year, in Winston-Salem, David and I trained with the Charlotte Division 2 wheelchair basketball team to keep up on our skills. The Rolling Razorbacks were able to fly me to the tournaments to play for the Razorbacks, but I only got to practice with them once before their season started.

Although things were going fairly well, I was already feeling compelled to search for new options. During the first nine months of my career, I had already used my seven weeks of paid vacation for competitions and training events. On top of that, I was asked by my bosses to sign off on paperwork completed by a previous salesperson.

I didn't feel comfortable with their request, because I knew of cases where people had gone to jail for falsifying paperwork.

I realized what implications there may be if errors were made on someone else's watch. I refused to sign the paperwork and told my bosses that I would not comply with any requests to put my name on work that wasn't my own.

I was called in the following morning and informed that my territory had been given to another salesman and that I would now begin working in a new territory where they currently had no marketing presence. I couldn't believe it. I had worked really hard to establish relationships with customers in my first territory, and now I would have to start from the beginning in an area of the country where no one knew of their small company. Was this a gift in disguise? Perhaps.

That same week, my girlfriend gave me the "ultimatum." She was ready to settle down and thought I was the right person for her. She wanted to get married. We had been dating for five years—she was ready to make a commitment or move on. Was this also a gift in disguise? Perhaps.

The new territory assignment, the girlfriend, and the looming tryouts for the 2000 Paralympic Games were enough stress to make me stop and seriously consider the direction my life was taking and what I was going to do about it. I wasn't spending the time I knew it would take to make the US National team and I knew I had to make some changes to keep the priorities in my life straight.

So what did I do? I quit my job, answered my girlfriend's ultimatum with "Let's both move on," and made the move back to Wisconsin where I felt I would have the best setup to train for the National team. Several of my teammates were still there, as well as my family, and it felt like the right decision to move home.

After returning home to Whitewater, I rededicated myself to my passion of wheelchair basketball. I started training like I had in college—six hours every single day, pushing myself to get back into shape. I began to find myself again. I was joined by several old teammates and together we practiced for the upcoming Paralympic year.

My hard work paid off. After multiple tryouts, I was named one of the twelve players to participate on the 2000 Paralympic team in Sydney, Australia. It was my first Paralympic experience, and I was so happy and proud to represent the United States abroad.

Wheelchair basketball began in the United States and was founded by World War II Veterans with Disabilities. The first game was thought to be played in California on November twenty-fifth in 1946. At first, the medical community had mixed opinions on having disabled people play sports. Many feared the inherent risks. However, the Veterans ignored that advice and because of that we have wheelchair basketball.

Founded in 1948 for World War II veterans with spinal cord injuries, the Paralympic Games became an international competition that focused on the athlete's unique abilities rather than their disabilities. There were a total of four hundred athletes from twenty-three different countries. At the 2008 Paralympic Games, there were four thousand two hundred athletes from one hundred and forty-eight different countries. It wasn't until 1976 that events for athletes with non-spinal cord injuries took place. In 1988, it was decided that whichever country was selected to host the Olympic Games was also to host the Paralympic Games. The Paralympic Games was named for their mission to parallel the Olympic Games—literally combining the word *Para,* which is Latin for *with,* and the word *Olympic.*

Paralympic basketball in particular is governed by the International Wheelchair Basketball Federation (IWBF). The IWBF regulates all facets of the game. Many of the rules are exactly the same as for able-bodied basketball players. For example, the basket height remains ten feet. The competition is open to athletes with varying disabilities. Many, like me, are amputees, but some have had a brain injury or stroke, while others may have had a spinal cord injury, partial paralysis, or orthopedic disabilities.

Before Sydney, I attended several intensive training camps and team competitions. My team gathered for Paralympic processing at the Colorado Springs Olympic Training Center, and we were all given their Team USA gear. Each team member was given a suit and then it was tailored for the opening ceremonies in Sydney. It felt surreal to be a part of such a huge moment.

The Team USA wheelchair team arrived in Sydney a week before the games began to acclimate to the time change and to have time to practice as a team. Each player had learned the plays at home, but now it was time to put all of the components together and work as a team.

The Paralympic Games took place two weeks after the Olympic Games ended and the wheelchair basketball team was housed at the same Olympic village. The USA basketball team was given a whole house within the village and I was once again paired with David as a roommate.

The opening ceremonies were fantastic. Team USA marched together—along with teams from other countries—in front of eighty thousand spectators. I had chills thinking of all the work I had done to prepare for this moment and how proud I was to be a part of such a monumental athletic event.

Team USA did well in their first few rounds and all of the games were sold out with twenty-five thousand people in the stands. When we were in the crossover finals playing Canada, the game went into overtime and we lost.

I was devastated, as was the rest of the team. We had gold medals in sight and now we were gearing up for the game that would define who went home with the Bronze. We were to play Great Britain.

The game was very difficult. Points went back and forth, and with barely any time left in the game, we were down by two points. With literally seconds remaining, we got a loose rebound and made a long three point shot as the clock expired. We had bronze! While it wasn't the gold medal, we were happy to be coming home with some hardware. Team USA stood on the podium among the best in the world.

After returning home to Whitewater to resume normal life, I debated what my next step would be. Should I get another "real job" so I could train and play ball, or maybe go back to school for a graduate degree?

Shortly after I got back, I received an email from a man in Spain who had seen me play in Sydney. He wanted to invite me to Spain for tryouts with his team in Madrid. He was the director on a professional team that—if interested enough in my skill set—would offer me a contract to play for salary.

I was intrigued by the opportunity. It was hard to imagine that I could play basketball, full-time, as a career. I replied to the email requesting a ticket to fly to Madrid for tryouts. At the very least, this would be a chance to travel to Spain, all expenses paid.

He had told me that he would be at the Madrid airport waiting to pick me up when the plane landed. When I exited the plane, I waited for my wheelchair. They usually brought it to me right away upon exiting the plane, but this time, the wheelchair was nowhere to be found. I asked around to see if any of the flight attendants or airport personnel spoke English. Finally I was able to speak with an agent who told me it had most likely been taken to the baggage claim. Assuming maybe they just did things differently in Spain, I went to baggage claim. My luggage appeared, but the wheelchair was gone.

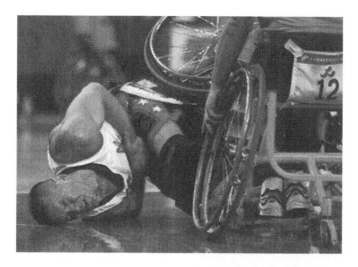

Above: 2000 Paralympic Games in Sydney, Australia. Sometimes life knocks you down.

Right: Goodwill training camp for the Chinese National Team. Playing around with my first wheelchair basketball coach.

DAY 5: MOVING TO SPAIN

"You cannot dream yourself into a character:
you must hammer and forge yourself into one."
–Henry D. Thoreau

I found my clothing bag, but still had no sign of the wheelchair. After searching the other baggage claim and coming up empty handed, I started to get worried. I thought I had lost the one possession that mattered most as I started out on this new adventure.

I finally found an Iberian flight employee who spoke broken English. The man escorted me to their office, where I tried my best—through the language barrier—to explain what had happened. I had left the wheelchair at the door of the outbound airplane and was given a baggage claim ticket they'd promised would match my wheelchair in Madrid. They looked up the baggage claim number, but couldn't locate it. They requested I fill out a lost baggage form with a description of the wheelchair and told me all they could do was contact me if and when they found it.

This was slightly problematic: I had no idea where I was staying, the phone number where they could reach me, or any details about how they could deliver the wheelchair. Instead, I decided to write down all of the Iberian contact info so I could hound them until they tracked down my extremely valued possession.

I continued on through the airport, passed through the remaining immigrations checkpoints, and went to the designated place to meet my team contact. There were a lot of people holding signs and I felt confident soon I would be approached by my contact. I had never met him, but I figured he had seen pictures of me from random basketball articles. I scanned the crowd, hoping to make eye contact with someone who would recognize me.

The crowd began to clear, and still, no one approached me. I realized at that moment that, to a stranger, I looked like everyone else. I was maybe a few inches taller, but I had worn pants to travel, so nobody knew I was missing a leg. I had banked on having my wheelchair, which would have been a dead giveaway for my contact to spot me. Instead, I decided to go change into some shorts so maybe I could stick out.

After changing, I waited another hour and still no one showed. I began to think maybe there had been some mistake. Two hours had passed by the time we were scheduled to meet, but all I could do was wait. I am not the best at details. I hadn't thought to make any sort of backup plan as I had been told everything would be arranged *for* me. I couldn't find a computer to check my email. Maybe something had come up at the last minute?

I waited another hour and finally decided to exchange some money and call a friend in the US to get online and check my email for me. The friend did so obligingly, but I had no new emails from anyone in Spain.

Three hours after I had shown up at the meeting place, a man approached me and asked if I was Jeff Glasbrenner. It was him! His excuse was they had been held up in traffic, and then he mumbled some Spanish, which I didn't catch except for, "No pasa nada," meaning "no worries." This became my new motto while in Spain.

What was "no worries" to him had been a big worry to me, but I soon learned I would have to flex a little to mingle in the Spanish culture. I did my best to forget about it. We exchanged friendly greetings and discussed what to do about my missing wheelchair. All we could do was wait and hopefully hear something from the airline.

Fundosa ONCE—my new team—was a team with rich history in Wheelchair basketball in Europe. The foundation and team were, and are still, funded by the ONCE lottery system. ONCE was originally founded to help the blind have a more accessible life. They provided public services, like curb cuts and pedestrian beep signals at cross walks, and also helped the visually disabled find gainful employment. Later on, they expanded the scope to include most disabilities, which is how the basketball team was started.

A percentage of every lottery ticket sold would go into the ONCE organization to help change or impact the lives of someone with a disability. My new teammates either sold lottery tickets or worked for ONCE. They were also paid a stipend to play on the team. Your value to the team was reflected in your pay.

Another foreign athlete on my new team, a Frenchman, was also staying on campus where they'd decided to house me. He could speak French and Spanish, but no English. Unfortunately, the Spanish I had learned on my flight overseas didn't lend itself much to conversation. My trip was definitely off to an interesting start.

The next day, I was scheduled to meet with the team for practice. There was a big problem, though: still no wheelchair. I went and met the players, but had to watch from the sidelines on day one and day two.

On day three they found me a wheelchair that was far too big with no waist strap to hold me in case I got knocked over. They wanted me to play to see if I would be a good fit for the team. I wasn't accustomed to this disproportional chair though, and was very hesitant to get on the court. It made me feel big and sloppy. From what I had seen playing on the US national team, these guys were good, but not the best. I wheeled on the court in my oversized chair and actually had a great practice.

Afterward, I grabbed my Spanish dictionary and tried to make some conversation with one of the players. I had been impressed with a move this guy had done on the court and I wanted to know how he was moving in and getting a score every time. I stumbled through the questions in Spanish and he was very happy to try and communicate back.

The following day, my new friend brought a Spanish-to-English dictionary for himself and began asking questions in

English about how I was making some of my better moves. Although we spoke two different languages, the language of basketball was common ground for us to hit it off.

After playing with the team for a few days, I was offered a contract. I responded that I didn't want to talk contracts until they could see me play in my own wheelchair, which *finally* arrived the next day. I was so thrilled to have it back. It was like I had been trying to run in someone else's shoes, and now I had shoes that fit *just right*. I brought my chair to practice the next day and dominated.

I was told after practice that day that I would have a meeting with the coaches and the manager the next morning. They offered me a great contract, which I decided to take. I would be paid to live and play basketball in Spain for the next year, traveling with their team, and competing in basketball tournaments all over Europe.

Thrilled about this new opportunity, I celebrated with my new French friend and teammate—with my Spanish dictionary in my back pocket. Since my flight back to the US wasn't for another three days, I drove with him to his home in Paris and spent the next few days touring Paris and all its sites—the Eiffel Tower, Notre Dame, Versailles, and other fabulous places. I realized how fortunate I was to get to do what I loved. This was *indeed* a gift. I was beginning to have a real love for travel and seeing the world and this new opportunity on the Spanish team would provide me so many chances for that.

Upon my return to Spain, I learned that coaches and training in Spain were a little different than in the US. When I signed my contract, I assumed I would be playing with the same players that were at tryouts. That was not the case as most of the players were on a year-to-year contract.

When I returned, the team directors decided to go in a new direction. They hired a new coach and got rid of five players—three of whom had been in the starting lineup. They replaced those players with me and another young man from the British National team. He was from the team we had defeated to win the Bronze medal at the 2000 Paralympic Games.

Although I wasn't crazy about the idea of playing with my former rival, we became friends fast. He and I were assigned as roommates in a team apartment. We had totally different personalities. From my coach in college, I had learned to be punctual. In fact, I hated being late. My new roommate, on the other hand, was never on time. It wouldn't have been such a big deal, except that he and I had to share a car to get to practices and events. I was constantly waiting on him—waiting on him to leave for practice, waiting on him to go get some grub, or waiting on him to catch a flight.

After a few months of playing together, he had to leave the team to go back to England to seek treatment for a pressure sore. This was hard on me because he was one of the more talented players on the team and was an English-speaking friend. A lot of the pressure now fell on *me* to make the winning moves. Even though I am always up for a challenge, to win at that level I knew I couldn't do it on my own.

Despite being short-handed, Team ONCE actually had a fairly successful year. In 2001 ONCE qualified in Utrecht, Netherlands for the Euro Cup Championships. The Euro Cups were the highest level of tournaments for wheelchair basketball in Europe. I was named the MVP. Euro Cup games brought the best of the best from numerous countries. Each team's goal was to be one of the top eight teams to qualify for the Euro Cup Championship.

In 2001, the Euro Cup was held in Pescara, Italy. My team won our first round and had a great game against the former three-time Euro Cup champions from Meaux, France. We lost by two points. I was devastated by the defeat. This was the first time my new girlfriend, Elizabeth, had seen me cry. ONCE ended up finishing in fourth, but I won the MVP award again.

Two other major tournaments took place that year—the Kings Cup and the Campeonato de Espana. Again, my team had made the final eight to qualify for both. At the King's Cup, Fundosa, ONCE finished second place, and I was yet *again* awarded the MVP.

These cup games were well attended by the European crowd. Sometimes there would even be live music and fans would travel to watch their favorite teams play. This was very different from wheelchair basketball in the United States. I had grown accustomed to seeing only people I knew in the stands— the families and friends of the players. In Europe, there was a true following. The Cup games were noted in the paper and the players were interviewed often by reporters—very different from what I knew back home.

In fact, the whole structure of wheelchair basketball was different in the US than in Europe. The USA teams played wheelchair basketball in a tournament fashion, playing a lot of games over the course of a weekend. A team may only have five tournaments scheduled, but there were a lot of games within those five tournaments. The reason for this mostly had to do with the physical expanse of the US. The tournaments were further away for teams, and since the sport was less funded than in Europe, it was cost effective to have fewer tournaments.

On the European side, there was only one big game a week, but each team played a game every week. The varied structure of the playing schedule made training and competing very different than in the States. In the US I was used to having a weekly team practice that would last around two hours. Sometimes players wouldn't show due to work or family—or lack of commitment— so we would only practice with five or six players. It was an amateur sport in the US—players received no direct salary from the team. Most of them maintained full-time jobs.

In Spain, I practiced with the team four days a week for at least two and a half hours. We played every Saturday or Sunday, and every player showed up to all the practices, because it was their job. We were professional athletes that were paid to perform. The level of commitment was on a different level—one that I respected and fit in with quite well.

ONCE had a team doctor, massage therapists, a head coach, assistant coach, and a team manager. The team manager spoke English fluently. The rest hardly spoke English at all—the coach included. At first, I had to have the manager translate what the coach was saying during practice and especially during games when he was calling for plays. As my time in Spain progressed, I learned more Spanish from being around the language and studying some on my own.

All in all, I had a great start to my year in Europe and had meshed well with my team. ONCE finished an overall second in the Spanish league that year, behind the team with the best regular team record. I was named the Spanish league's MVP for the entire Cup series—an incredible distinction and honor.

2002 World Championship

That same year, I was selected to be Captain of the US National Team—an honor and product of hard work and great results on the court. I flew back to the US from Spain on my own dime to try out for the US National team.

In wheelchair basketball, the two highest-ranking tournaments are the World Championships and the Paralympics—they are held every other two years. In 2002, my goal as Captain was to qualify Team USA for the World Championships at the Para Pan Am games.

The 2002 qualifying tournament was held in Vitoria, Brazil, a third world part of Brazil. The crowds at the games were high in number and electric. The top three teams would qualify for the World Championships. Team USA did its job and placed second to the Canadians. We were going to Japan!

The World Championships in 2002 were hosted in Kitakyushu, Japan. Team USA arrived a week before the tournament to begin to acclimate to the fourteen- hour time change. This was my first trip to Japan. My first observation was the sheer *number* of people. Everywhere we traveled the streets were packed.

Walking around in the rush hour of people I was very glad I was tall, because I could find the path of least resistance.

That week of training equipped Team USA for the battle we were about to enter. The team meshed well and practice sessions were positive as teammates rallied to make their plays seamless. The opening ceremonies were spectacular. The King and Queen of Japan attended.

Our first game of the World Championships was against Great Britain. It was a very tough, physical game. We lost in overtime, seventy-seven to seventy-two. This was *not* the way we wanted to start out our bid for the Gold Medal at the World Championships. We regrouped as a team and went on to win the rest of the games in our pool.

Our first quarterfinals game was a *tough* game against Germany. The Half time score was in our favor, but not by much: thirty-three to thirty-two. We ended up beating Germany, seventy to fifty-seven. I played well, scoring fourteen points and grabbing fifteen rebounds.

As fate would have it, our Gold medal game was against Great Britain. This was where it counted. So far, they had been the only team to beat us, and that was in overtime. The game didn't start out very well. We were down eight to zero in the first couple of minutes. After a timeout and some mental fortitude, we regrouped and got in our groove that we all knew we had. At half-time the score was thirty-nine to thirty-two. It was a back and forth battle, but we ended up *World Champions* with a score of seventy-four to sixty-one.

2002 World Championship Gold Medal team in Japan.

DAY 6: MEETING ELIZABETH

"When one door of happiness closes, another opens,
but often we look so long at the closed door that we do not
see the one
that has been opened for us."
–Helen Keller

Early in the spring of 2000, I was living at home in Wisconsin, heavy into training for the Sydney Olympics. In April I was contacted by my friend, David, who at the time ran the sports program for children with disabilities in Charlotte, North Carolina.

He called to ask if I would like to participate in a huge fundraising event to benefit their sports program. This particular fundraiser targeted distinguished, disabled athletes to raise funds for the program by riding a hand-crank bike two hundred miles from Charlotte, North Carolina, to Myrtle Beach, South Carolina—a challenge that was right up my alley.

I was immediately on board, provided they would fly me in to Charlotte to participate.

That didn't fly well with the event organizer—a young woman in her twenties named Elizabeth Smiley. The whole effort was to raise money for the Children's Hospital, not to spend money to get the athletes there. David told me that he gave it his best pitch to fly me in for this event. But, according to David, Elizabeth said that I could pay my own way to Charlotte to help these children.

Elizabeth was born and raised in Little Rock, Arkansas. She went to Washington University in St. Louis for college, and then moved on to Colorado after graduation to work at The National Sports Center for the Disabled in Winter Park. She spent the first part of her post-collegiate career working around children with disabilities and eventually found herself doing event planning for this wonderful organization.

She had made the drastic move from Colorado to Charlotte for a boyfriend who broke up with her six months later—another gift in disguise? She was fortunate to find a great job doing fundraising for the Children's Hospital. Elizabeth was given this particular fundraiser because of her previous experience at the National Sports Center for the Disabled. This "Cycle to the Sea" fundraiser was a huge event for her to pull together as all their participants were disabled and were required to fundraise to play a part.

The day the event began, the weather was ominous, and just as the event organizers had everyone rallied to start, police car escorts in line, and media ready to cover the event, the rain began pouring down. The event was set to start from a local Wal-Mart—one of their sponsors—and we were to have police escorts ride with us the first five miles, until we got off the busier roads.

With the rain impairing visibility and the athletes already being lowered to the ground on their hand crank bikes, she had to make an executive call. For the safety of the participants, she decided to move the start five miles further down the course where the roads were not so heavily trafficked. They began loading up the vehicles and asked the media cameras to reposition the start. I can only assume this was a frustrating and disappointing moment for Elizabeth.

It was at this moment that she got her first taste of me. I rolled up to her car on my borrowed hand-crank bike as they were loading up and in all seriousness stated, "I came here to ride two hundred miles, not a hundred and ninety-five."

Elizabeth recognized me as the guy that wanted the free ticket to the fundraiser—David had pointed me out to her the previous night at their kick-off party. Elizabeth looked me square in the face and replied with what looked like a fake smile, "Well, then you'd better get started riding around the parking lot to get your five miles in before we transition you to the new start line." She then turned back to her car and continued to pack up. I couldn't believe her audacity.

Stunned by her blunt response, I rolled away and immediately began riding my soaking wet bike laps around the parking lot before regrouping with the other riders. I have to admit, I was incensed with Elizabeth's response and confused that she didn't understand my desire to complete the whole two hundred miles.

The fundraiser lasted three days. At the end of each day, I rolled up to Elizabeth's car and asked if she could drive some of the participants somewhere to get dinner. She politely declined, reminding us we had dinner already organized. I got the feeling that she thought I just wanted special treatment.

At the after-party on the third day, Elizabeth was standing off to the side letting all the participants recount their numerous memories of the trek they had just made.

I stared at her until our eyes made contact. I smiled warmly and made my way over to her. Sounds cheesy, but it is true. "Do you realize I have been trying to flirt with you for three days?" I asked? Elizabeth gave out a cute giggle. According to her, my attempts at flirtation had apparently come across as nothing but arrogant demands. However, I suppose something about me left her smitten. She told me later that she had found me attractive from the moment she'd first seen me, but my attitude and our initial confrontation had turned her off. Now, after giving me a little time for conversation, she began to see I wasn't just a stubborn competitor—I had a softer side.

The day everyone left Myrtle Beach, I slipped Elizabeth my email address on a torn piece of paper. I desperately wanted to hear from her.

She emailed. She explained to me that it was not like a Southern girl to take that initiative, but I am so thankful she did. From there, we occasionally corresponded by email and phone. We lived in separate states, so we didn't get to see each other much. Elizabeth casually dated other people, as did I, but we never were able to get out of one another's minds.

Later that summer, I traveled to Sydney for the 2000 Paralympic Games and I called Elizabeth during an off-day. She sounded proud of me on the phone and said she was honored that I was thinking about her during this huge competition. When I returned to the states, we met a few times, but still nothing serious happened.

Phone conversations were becoming more regular, but I had just received another offer to move and play basketball in Madrid, while Elizabeth had just moved back home to Little Rock where she could be close to family and to take the opportunity to learn from her Dad in the business world.

Life had put us in two different places for the time being, and neither of us really seemed bothered by it. We were talking on the phone a lot and instant messaging one another on the computer.

One day, I told Elizabeth, "You should come visit me while I'm living over here." She promptly responded, "Don't say that if you really don't mean it, because I am a person that makes things happen." I bought her a plane ticket and she came to Madrid.

As she was getting ready to land in Madrid, Elizabeth recounts having a moment of panic, thinking, *What am I doing? I don't really know this guy that well. What if he's a weirdo, or better yet, what if he doesn't even show up to get me?* She told me that when I came around the corner at baggage claim, all of her fears were relieved. It was then that we both knew it was right.

A few nights into her trip, as we toasted drinks at a local Irish pub, I think the Guinness helped boost Elizabeth's confidence enough for her to finally ask me, "If we lived in the same town, do you think we would date?" I was puzzled by her question and responded, "I thought we *were* dating."

It was an exclusive relationship from there forward. Elizabeth returned to Spain numerous times over the next two years as I continued to play professionally in European Cups and tournaments.

During those visits, we lived an experience to be cherished forever. We explored the Spanish and the European countryside and truly got to know each other. We lived an adventure together as our long-distance relationship grew.

Elizabeth said I was the perfect boyfriend to date transcontinental, because I made communication work. Every day I called or emailed. As our relationship matured, this meant we were forced to be friends first, to really get to know each other. It was hard being apart, but at the same time, I was making a living doing what I loved and Elizabeth was building a career and we both got to travel to wonderful places every time she came to see me.

Knowing my history, I told her very early on, "I date people for like five years." To which she responded, "OK." I had experienced enough ultimatums from my last girlfriend, and I was very afraid of having to change my dream—that I was finally living—for a girl. I figured I would prepare Elizabeth up-front. I had come to trust her enough to know that her intentions were not to make me change.

Elizabeth and I complemented each other. I needed support, freedom, and trust from a girlfriend to be abroad full-time and attend to my commitments. Elizabeth was confident, easy-going, and wanted me to chase my dreams.

There were times in her visits that she had to be a real trooper. We often traveled a lot for games. Sometimes she would not even get to stay at the same hotel as me. At away games, wives and girlfriends were not allowed to be with the team, as the coaches were afraid the players would be distracted.

Elizabeth stayed with the other wives and girlfriends—none of whom spoke English—and then watched me play. She made new friends and quickly bought a pocket Spanish dictionary that went with her everywhere. She was flexible and independent. That was what I loved about her.

When we had free time together, we made the most of it. One of the most memorable trips was to Granada, where we decided to sign up for an authentic Flamenco dancing show. I paid for tickets at the hotel and we were told to meet in the lobby at 7 p.m.

We watched as the van that was supposed to take everyone filled to the brim and were told there was no room for us. The driver told us not to worry, that he would send a car to pick us up and follow behind.

About half an hour later, we were still waiting in the lobby when a random car pulled up to the curb. The driver said, "Get in!" There was no signage for the Flamenco show and the driver seemed to know about five English words, so we drove in silence.

We kept driving and driving. We were getting further away from the lighted city streets and onto the country roads, winding down private streets and allies. Elizabeth turned to me and said, "Have we been kidnapped, like on a Dateline special?" While scary and unsure, we still managed to laugh. *What had we done?*

After forty-five minutes of driving, the car delivered us to a stucco house that resembled a cave, the way it had been built into the landscape. We were escorted inside and were amazed at the beautiful interior.

It was an intimate setting, the inside adorned with traditional Spanish décor and color. We had arrived in time to watch and listen to the amazing dance and music.

We also had more stressful, realistic days, like Barcelona, where we had our first real fight. Elizabeth had been given a stick shift rental car, which she hadn't exactly mastered as we drove our way through crowded streets. It didn't help that I didn't believe in reading maps and was supposed to be helping Elizabeth navigate.

I had had enough of her bad driving. We finally pulled over to switch seats so I could drive and Elizabeth could navigate. I was accustomed to driving with my left foot, but with a clutch, I had to use my prosthetic leg to work the gas and brake. As

Elizabeth tried to find where we were on the map, I was doing my best, but stop-and-go traffic with a stick shift and a prosthetic right leg made for a very jerky ride.

Clearly our frustration level with each other was growing. When we decided to stop for lunch, I asked, "What do you want to eat?" Elizabeth asked, "What do they have?" She couldn't read any of the Spanish items on the menu.

I fired back with, "Just tell me what you want and I'll figure it out." She said she didn't know what she wanted, because she could only decide *that* once she knew what the options were. We were both frustrated from being cooped up on a bouncy, nauseating car ride. That day tested our patience and our relationship limits.

Most of the time, we ended up at the Hard Rock Café. We could both read the menu for one, and it was one of the places where I could get "American" food and a chocolate brownie dessert. I have a huge sweet tooth.

Early in 2002—after we'd been dating exclusively abroad for about six months—there was an entire week when I didn't talk to Elizabeth. She emailed me, called me, left messages, and I just didn't respond.

It wasn't like me to not call or touch base through email. Elizabeth told me later that her worst fears took over. *Something had happened to me.* But then she realized someone from the team would have contacted her if that were the case, so the only other reason she could imagine for me to ignore her messages was that I didn't want to date her anymore.

Finally, after a week of silence, she called and left me a message simply saying, "I just want to know if you're OK. Can you please just call or email to let me know you're all right?"

So, I responded. The conversation was slightly heated. I played it cool. "So what's wrong?" I asked.

Elizabeth responded, "The only reason our relationship is working, is because you have been a good communicator. I'm not interested in having a long-distance relationship with someone who is not going to talk to me for weeks at a time."

I laughed and said, "I just needed to see if I missed you. If I removed myself from our conversations, I would know whether I truly missed you being a part of my life."

Her first response was: "Seriously?" She didn't understand—and in retrospect who could blame her—but thankfully decided to give me the benefit of the doubt. I *had* truly missed her. She asked me point blank, "Are you going to need to see if you miss me again anytime soon?"

"I promise, I won't need to do that experiment ever again." She was the one.

In May of 2002, Elizabeth flew to Madrid, similar to every other trip she made abroad—weary and jetlagged. Our usual routine was to try and keep her up the following day (the plane arrived at 8:30 a.m. Madrid time) so she could quickly acclimate to the new time zone.

She hated being jetlagged, and we had decided what was best was for her to get off the plane and immediately take a short nap to refresh herself for the day ahead. We arrived at my small apartment and she was headed to bed for a rest.

I stopped her in her tracks, though. With my scared, serious face, I said, "There's something important I need to talk to you about."

Exhausted, Elizabeth told me later she automatically thought the worst. I had allowed her to fly all the way to Spain just to break up with her. What else could possibly be so important right at that moment? It didn't help that I was scared to death, since my eyes were wide and my smile was gone.

Her cheeks turned red. Despite waiting for me to drop the break-up bomb, she calmly replied, "Honey, you can talk to me about anything."

"We've been through a lot, and you mean the world to me. You've traveled all over the place just to come be with me, and you've loved me, while giving me the freedom to do what I love." I pulled a ring out of my pocket. "Will you marry me?"

Elizabeth's fears quickly turned to joy. She had no hesitation. She knew she wanted to marry me. All the obstacles—the fact that we'd never lived in the same city, that I lived in another country, that her family didn't even really know me—all those things were minor details at that moment. We both knew in our hearts that we would figure it out.

After giving me an enthusiastic yes, Elizabeth reminded me of my warning. "I thought you dated people for like five years?"

I smiled and told her, "You're different. I know you're the one for me."

Soon after, I wrapped up my European Cup tournaments and decided to move to Little Rock where Elizabeth had established a good career and her family resided. We had to figure out how to live in the same city, and in the same house. All I needed to know was that the city had a good climate, an airport, and Elizabeth. Little Rock met all three.

We decided to get married in October of 2002. We both wanted a destination wedding. Elizabeth had never really meshed with the idea of a full-blown southern wedding with the huge white dress, the music, the crowd, and the pomp and circumstance.

It was a hard decision to make, because I had a huge family, and Elizabeth's parents were divorced, so there were two sides to include. Even a small wedding would have consisted of at least fifty people, and that excluded our friends. All of it seemed stressful, so we decided to run away and get married in Hope Town, Bahamas, with just a few of our closest friends.

We knew it would be hard to explain to our families, but it's what we both wanted. Everyone kept saying to Elizabeth, "I can't believe you don't want your Daddy to walk you down the aisle!"

Elizabeth loves her Dad very much, but she knew her Dad wanted her to do what would make her the happiest. Every bride and groom should be able to decide what they wanted at their wedding.

We bought plane tickets for six friends and ourselves and scheduled the wedding at a small Methodist church in Hope Town on Saturday, October twenty-sixth at 4 p.m.

The little church was exactly what we had pictured. The back windows faced the ocean, and the sea breeze blew through the doors with refreshing vigor. It was perfect.

That Monday before we left town, the preacher—who also happened to be the town baker—called Elizabeth to inform her there had been some unexpected changes. There was a member of Bahamian royalty who had decided they wanted to use the church on Saturday the twenty-sixth and they were forced to bump us to another time. We could either have it earlier that Saturday morning, or Friday the twenty-fifth at 4 p.m.

After discussing it, we decided we wanted to keep the wedding and meal in the afternoon and evening, so we chose Friday. We had received several gifts engraved with our wedding date as the twenty-sixth, but we just laughed about it and used the gifts anyway. My mom was actually relieved—she had felt horrible because she had engraved, in advance, a beautiful silver platter mistakenly for October twenty-fifth. Turns out, she was the only one who got the day right.

So the wedding was moved to the twenty-fifth, but all the other preparations remained intact. The preacher handled everything for us. He was the baker and made our cake. His wife handled the music. His daughter arranged the flowers.

As I walked to the church to wait for the ceremony, I began to have moments of fear. "What if she doesn't show? What if she changed her mind? Does my breath smell bad?" I loved this woman so much and couldn't wait to be her husband.

When Elizabeth started down the aisle, my fears subsided. My sisters had tears running down their faces. Standing in front of the big windows overlooking the ocean, the preacher began to talk. He told a beautiful story about two islands, joined by water, and how much that was akin to marriage. "To make a marriage work," he continued, "you both have to remain individuals, but you are now joined together."

The ceremony was so beautiful, intimate and meaningful. Standing in front of Elizabeth telling her how much I loved her and hearing how much she loved me in return is a moment I will never forget. Dinner following the ceremony was at the Hope Town Harbor Lodge. That restaurant has the best coconut grouper on the planet. During dinner, she asked the group, "What is the best marriage advice you could give us?"

All our friends present were married or had been in a relationship with someone for over a decade. One couple's advice particularly stood out. It was from friends from Elizabeth's college time in St. Louis. They said, "Marriage is never fifty/fifty. You have to go into each day willing to give one hundred percent, because on any given day, one or both of you will not be able to give even fifty."

We took that to heart, and after years of being married to each other, that advice resounds in our hearts and minds as true.

After spending the next day celebrating with our friends, snorkeling, boat riding, hanging out on the beach, and sipping on cocktails—exactly what we had envisioned for a wedding—our friends left to come home while we remained a few more days for our "honeymoon."

Soon after our return to Little Rock, I received an offer to play on a wheelchair basketball team in Rome. We had just been married, and immediately, another opportunity for me to move abroad had fallen into our laps.

We talked a long time. The opportunity was for eight months, and I could negotiate trips for Elizabeth to come and visit me on a regular basis.

At first Elizabeth had reservations. She was in the beginning stages of starting a business with her brother. It didn't make sense for us, long-term, to put that on hold for eight months. We had barely begun our life together and faced a tough decision. We knew I would travel, but didn't expect to live apart our first year of being married. But, we also weighed how amazing our time had been when we were traveling in Spain. We could have the same experience, but in a new place—Italy.

For eight months, it didn't seem right that she should abandon her dreams of starting this new business and move to Rome with me. Could we have both?

What most people would struggle with, we made work. We understood each other well, and Elizabeth gave me the freedom to go guilt-free and have the chance of a lifetime. She supported me one hundred percent. I supported her decision to stay in Little Rock and work on her business. When I accepted the position on the team, Elizabeth and I agreed that several plane tickets had to be part of the deal. That's how our relationship was founded: in a mutual understanding of one another's dreams, a deep trust and respect for each other, and the attitude of each giving one hundred percent to the goals we shared.

In late 2003, I returned home to the United States and to my beautiful wife. Overseas was great, but I was ready to live in the same city as my wife. Also, there were a few more championships I wanted to check off my list. After winning the EuroCup with the Italian team, I was eager to try and win its equivalent—a Final Four championship in the United States with the NWBA (National Wheelchair Basketball Association). I had been to a championship game with Arkansas in 1998, but we lost. When I got back to Little Rock, I had a couple of teams interested in my talent. The good thing about playing with the NWBA is that I could actually live at home and travel to my team (in earlier years this was allowed, but not now). My decision was to play with the Denver Nuggets. Denver had always held a special place in my heart from all of our family trips, and it was a new team to the Division 1 level.

A good friend of mine was also to join the Denver team. His unselfish playing style allowed me the opportunity to "pick and roll" with him throughout the season. This style enabled me to get to the basket and score with ease. It is important that the two people working the "pick and roll" understand what the other person is doing. He helped the team, often at the expense of scoring himself. We worked well with each other. We were true friends on and off the court. We only lost three games the whole year. Each of those three losses were to the same team—the Dallas Mavericks. Going into the Final Four tournament, the games were split with three wins apiece.

At the same time, I was learning to be an at home husband. Elizabeth and I had decided we needed to put new sod down at our house. Of course *I* wasn't going to pay to have that done. I could do that. There was two weeks before the Final Four tournament started. It was a big undertaking, but I was up for the challenge.

The first step was top soil. When the dump truck delivered and dumped the top soil in our driveway, the reality of what I had undertaken set in. Our house at the time was not built on the level, so I had to haul the topsoil up a hill with a wheelbarrow. I worked about ten hours a day for two days—on my feet, loading the top soil in the wheelbarrow, and carting it to the area to be dropped off. The second day my stump started to hurt, but I was half finished with the topsoil, so I powered through. That second night, my stump had swollen up to three times its normal size. I also had a fever. This is an amputee's worst nightmare—a blood infection in your stump.

The next morning my leg started draining blood and pus in massive amounts from the open sores that had been created by my stubbornness to finish this job. I went to the Emergency Room, but the infection had already set in. I was given antibiotics and was told to stay off my leg and rest. That wasn't a problem, because there was no way my prosthetic was going to fit on this swollen monster. My leg was massive. The only problem was that the sod was delivered that morning. We had a couple thousand dollars worth of sod in my front driveway. I am not good at asking for help or at giving up. I started laying the sod on my crutches and knees with Elizabeth's help. It wasn't the fastest process, but it was progress.

That evening, my problem-solving wife came to the rescue with friends and family. The next couple of days I spent in bed recovering from the infection, while our friends and family finished our yard. During this time, I was unable to train for basketball for a week. That was the longest time I had gone without playing ball in several years. I was still worn out from the antibiotics and from the yard job. The Final Four was looming and I was very fearful that I wouldn't have a great performance, because of my condition.

That year the Final Four was located in Phoenix, Arizona. Our team arrived two days before the games. During team practice, I was drained and didn't have the energy to play well. However, the rest of the team was looking great. The Final Four semi-final game was against the local Phoenix team. They were a solid team, but we had no problem with them all year. I played well—considering I didn't have much energy—and scored twenty-five points. The Dallas Mavericks had their semi-final game against the Milwaukee Bucks. The Mavericks went unchallenged as well. This set the stage for the two best teams of the season to face off the next day.

I was still talking my antibiotics at the time of the final and still very weak. My leg still didn't fit, so I brought my every-day wheelchair to get around instead of crutches to save a little energy. The gym was packed with spectators.

Before the game, my coach came up to me when I was stretching. He said, "I know you are not feeling the best, but today is my birthday. It would be the most incredible birthday if we could just win this game."

I really liked playing for this coach. He was very open to input and very passionate and competitive. I thought to myself, *Yeah, let's win this for his birthday.* My juices began to flow and I was ready. Sometimes I need a little push.

They made the announcement of the starting line-ups and I remember being really excited for the game to begin. The opening tip off, I lost the ball at the jump. The first five minutes, I didn't get a chance to touch the ball and we were down twelve to four.

Then something in me clicked. I started demanding the ball and making my moves to the basket. It was like I was on Autopilot. I was making moves with or without picks and scoring with ease against some of the best players in the world. The Mavericks had won three championships in a row coming into this game. It was a very balanced team with a lot of experience playing together. When our team missed a shot, I was in the right position, got the rebound, and put the ball in the hole. At the end of the half, I had scored thirty-one points. I believe the score was tied or very close at half time.

During half time, I was exhausted. My teammates kept coming up and asking me how many points I had scored. I responded I had no clue but it was a close game.

The NWBA videotaped the game. It videoed the Mavericks head coach saying, "It doesn't matter if Glas scores sixty points, all we have to do is contain the other players."

The third period started off with more of the same. I stayed hot and in the zone. At the start of the fourth period, the Mavericks started full court pressing me to slow up my scoring. It wasn't effective, because my teammates came back up the court and freed me off for the pick. Then, one of my teammates hit a big three point shot and all of sudden the entire team began to believe we could win.

With about eight minutes in the game, I was still on fire. I made a strong move to the basket for an easy layup, when out of nowhere a player from the Dallas Mavericks jumped out of his chair and almost tackled me to the floor. It was ruled a flagrant foul and I landed on my shooting shoulder. Shock and hurt set in. I collected myself and went to the line to shoot two free throws. I was in pain and missed both shots. It was the first two shots I had missed from the foul line in that game.

We got the ball at half court because of the flagrant foul and we scored. After a few minutes, I started to regain my composure and was determined to finish this game as we had started it. We ended up pulling away the score at the end with a few free throws.

The Denver Nuggets were the Division 1 NWBA Champions, winning one hundred and ten to ninety-nine. I was named MVP of the Championships and scored a record sixty-three points with twenty-seven rebounds. I broke the previous scoring record and interviews came my way. They asked me what I was feeling, and all I could say was that I felt like I was in a zone where I could do no wrong. The reporter also asked if it was just my lucky day. I responded, "It was a great day, but, it wasn't luck. It was seven years of hard work that made this day a reality. When training, you train for these days to happen. I am just happy that being in the zone happened on the most important basketball day—a championship."

After all of the team celebrated on the court, I went up to my coach and said, "Happy Birthday Coach!"

He looked at me and was all smiles. "Today is not my birthday. I just needed you to focus on something else—a little extra challenge to seal the deal." Today this is still our little joke.

Next on my list was the 2004 Paralympic Games in Athens, Greece. This was my second Paralympics. It was a rebuilding year for Team USA. We played like the young/new team. We managed to win our pool. Then we had a crossover game against Great Britain. We had played them many times throughout the year and had done well against them, however we did not win every time. This game was a battle back and forth and we ended up losing our first crossover game. This loss put us in a consolation game against Japan for the seventh/eighth place game. Unfortunately, this was nowhere near that Gold medal we had trained for and dreamed of. We ended up beating Japan for the seventh place participation prize.

My family had made the long trip to Athens to see Team USA go for the Gold. I always tried to look at things in a positive way. With losing early, we got a lot of free time to explore Athens. Exploring Athens with my wife, mother, sisters, and in-laws was incredible. It allowed me to get a real experience of the rest of the Paralympic Games too—one I had not experienced before. We visited the Acropolis, Pantheon, and even made a trip to one of the Greek islands.

The whole USA contingency had to travel together back to the United States. As you might imagine, it is quite a process to load the luggage, equipment, wheelchairs, and athletes onto any one mode of transportation. We loaded several buses from the athletes' village and made our way to the airport. Our flight was then delayed for two hours. They started with all of the wheelchair users first so they could use the aisle chairs in a quicker fashion. They started loading thirty or so wheelchair chair users using the aisle chair to take the athlete to his seat. It was a long slow process. Then, there was an announcement that they had discovered something was wrong with the plane, and they stopped boarding until they knew more. We waited another hour and they made another announcement saying our flight had to be canceled and that we would all have another flight home twenty-four hours later. It was a nightmare. We all loaded up and went back to the Olympic village. The cleaning people had already stripped our beds so we didn't really have any sheets or blankets. Without a Gold, I just wanted to go back home. Now we were stuck in Athens. We had to repeat the same process the next day, but we finally made it home. I left those games feeling pretty empty, but hungry. Now I wanted that Gold even more...if that was possible.

Above: Wedding Day in Abaco, Bahamas
Below: Gavin, Jeff, Elizabeth and Grace

Above left: Elizabeth's first marathon – Marine Corps Marathon. I was so proud of her!
Above right: Little Rock Marathon – Team Access Your Inner Warrior – fundraiser for Access Schools

2004 Paralympic Games in Athens. Made the shot!

DAY 7: MY FIRST TRIATHLON

"Winning isn't everything, but wanting to win is."
–Vince Lombardi

When I first lost my leg in the farming accident, I remember crying to my dad about never being able to run or swim again. This was true for twenty-four years after that accident—I didn't run or swim.

One day in 2005, I saw the Ironman World Championships in Hawaii on TV. It is an hour or so long program on NBC. The competition took place in Kona, Hawaii. It showed the awesome back drop of the land and amazing stories of people doing whatever they could to get to the finish line. I watched as cameras showed athletes sweating, cramping, grabbing for water at rest-stops, and pushing to the finish line after hours and hours of racing. I sat enamored as the winner crossed the finish line in a sub-nine hour time, his body spent. I was mesmerized by the on-screen atmosphere that surrounded the Ironman Championships, and suddenly I knew I belonged there. It sparked in me a desire to see if I could push myself to *that* level of intensity.

I am a type A+ competitive kind of guy so, if I am going to do something, I am going to do it at the highest level. The next day, I looked up the Ironman World Championships on the internet. My search quickly revealed that it was a little harder than that one-hour program led you to believe. It is a 2.4 mile swim, a one hundred and twelve mile bike ride, and a 26.2 mile run— all in one day. They also have a time cut-off for all of the segments. Something about it stuck with me though.

Before my accident, I had lived for my weekly trip to the local swimming pool. My parents had taken the kids once a week during the summer to swim. It was my favorite activity, and one I dearly missed after my accident. I also ran as a kid. I came in second place in a school race a couple of months before I lost my leg and I had always wished for that second chance to try for first.

As thoughts of triathlons began to swirl through my head, I allowed myself to revisit how much I had loved running and swimming as a kid. Even though wheelchair basketball kept me strong, lean, and athletic, my exercise routine consisted of weights and practicing on the courts. I had never really thought that I might get to swim, bike, and run.

Watching that first Ironman left me in awe that people would and could choose to push themselves that hard. I'd seen several athletes with disabilities finish the event on TV, but this in itself wasn't what urged me to begin exploring triathlons. I simply wanted to swim, bike, and run. I did, however, begin to research how other amputees were making it happen.

My first assignment was finding the right hardware. I knew I would need some very special equipment. The swimming was a no-brainer. I could jump in the water without any sort of prosthetic, but the bike and run were a different story.

I visited every prosthetic company in Little Rock, asking questions about how I could get a custom-molded leg to use on the bike and run portions. The bike leg had to have a compatible attachment to clip-in to the pedal securely, and my running leg had to have enough spring in the joint of the foot to propel me forward, similar to the way a calf muscle would help push a runner off the ground.

After talking to a lot of prosthetists in Little Rock, I realized none of them made a biking or running leg for what I wanted to do. Most of their products were for the more mature in age and for basic function, not sport.

I ended up meeting a rep from a local prosthetic company. He was young, liked challenges, and was up on the latest methods of technology.

The prosthetist and I worked together to formulate my first running leg. When I put it on and gave it a test trial, memories began to soar through my mind of being eight and the freedom I once had. This leg made me feel limitless—like a complete, whole person.

I remember putting the leg on for a lap around the parking lot, and although I was speechless with how much fun it was to be able to run again, I was also completely exhausted in about two minutes.

It would take some time to build up the stamina required to use my disabled leg for sports again. All the muscles that were normal in my left leg had counterparts in my right leg that had atrophied. I knew how to run, but it was as though my muscles had forgotten.

After just a couple of minutes test-running the leg, I also developed a sore on my stump. Running motion and impact caused a new type of friction between where the leg attached to my limb, and I quickly understood this would be one of the many pains I would have to deal with to compete. It was a price I was gladly willing to pay for the joy of getting to run again.

I had already been cycling for a couple of months with my regular prosthetic leg. I was first inspired by Lance Armstrong. I loved being on the bike, and since Lance rode Trek, that's what my first bike was. My first road bike was a Trek 600, and I couldn't believe I would spend eight hundred and fifty dollars for a bike.

My admiration for Lance took us all the way to France to watch his "last" tour. We had an amazing time in Europe. We watched two stages of the Tour De France. We watched one of the finishing mountain stages in a small town and then tried to get back to Lourdes to watch the stage finish. As the riders went by we were amazed with the whole race, and we got to see Lance go by in Yellow. We quickly jumped in the car with the plan of getting back to watch the finish. What you don't see on TV watching the Tour is all the people—everywhere, all the time. Streets are blocked off and it's very much a mob scene the whole time.

We were stuck in traffic and all of a sudden we could hear sirens blazing, and behind us the police were leading the parade of team cars racing back to the finish. We were at the front of the barricade, held back by police. The police motioned us to move forward to let the team cars by. Then there was a break in the car line up and my wife calls out, "Just go!" My sister was driving and hit the gas. We were now in the middle of the team car procession racing back to the finish at speeds nearing one hundred miles per hour. The team cars had their team logos, extra bikes, and wheels on top. We were in our midsized grey rental. People were cheering for their favorite teams as we passed. Other team cars were passing us and looking at us like "what gives?"

Then the Euskaltel-Euskadi (Orbea) team passed us and motioned for us to just come along. We made a dash with them. The whole time we saw police on their radios talking and even some pointing at us as we whizzed past them. We made it very close to the finish and exited off on a small street and parked the car. After catching our breath and hoping we wouldn't get arrested, we made it to the finish and had an amazing day.

The next day we saw all of the riders of the Tour De France sign in for that day's stage. Seeing Lance Armstrong up close, warming up on his trainer before the stage was a dream come true. It was madness how many people wanted to see Lance and Sheryl Crow up close.

We also got to meet Lance's biggest rival—Jan Ulrich, from Germany. He was signing autographs. I feverishly searched for paper to have him sign. When I couldn't find any, I whipped off my leg and had him sign it. My leg was covered in stars and stripes at the time. He smiled and said, "I have never done that before." We also toured a few other countries on our trip: Switzerland, Austria, Germany, and Paris. We took the Euro rail train for most of our travels.

Now that my interest had changed from biking as a hobby to biking as a sport, I realized I would have to change my setup. For months, I had used my every-day walking leg and had ridden with flat pedals. This was great in terms of functionality, but I knew the current setup did not provide the stability or power transfer I would have if I could clip my prosthetic into the pedal.

A few months later, a fellow amputee gave me the bottom portion of an older cycling leg he was no longer using. Although it was a left foot and I needed a right, I thought it could be of use and disassembled the foot shell from the carbon fiber body of the leg. I drilled three holes in the bottom of the foot for attaching a cleat—mimicking the cleat hole pattern of a normal cycling shoe. He then made a carbon fiber socket for the body of the right prosthetic, and attached the two parts together. The result was a functional cycling leg. I could put on his prosthetic—now with a Keo LOOK cleat attached to the bottom—and clip in to my compatible pedal. Now, I was able to ride with more power and I didn't have to worry about my foot sliding off the pedal.

Swimming, biking, and running were now all in my grasp. After talking with a friend at the gym, I decided to do the Olympic distance triathlon—Memphis in May, 2005. This would be my first competition triathlon. This triathlon was fairly close to home, the course was flat, and the swim was a staggered-time-trial start so I wouldn't have to worry about dealing with the masses in the water.

Since I was still playing basketball at the time, I hadn't really trained. I just did all I could to squeeze in with my training schedule. Never before had I done all those distances—a fifteen hundred meter swim, a forty kilometer bike ride, and a ten kilometer run—in one day.

When the gun sounded, I was hopping toward the water in my bright yellow swim cap and began to experience a lot of doubt. *What I had gotten myself into?* After I got in the water, I got hit in the head by another swimmer and I remembered thinking, *I thought this was a non-contact sport!*

I was used to being knocked around on the basketball court, but in a lake? Finishing the swim felt like an eternity, but I got out of the water and hopped up the boat ramp where I had left my leg.

After attaching my leg, I looked up and had a moment of dread. There were fifteen hundred racers and I couldn't remember where my bike was. Rookie mistake. Luckily, I spotted my extra equipment—a cycling prosthetic stuck out in the crowd. I grabbed my bike and began walking it out of the transition area.

The only hill on the bike course was at the start. Elizabeth watched as several athletes rode the hill in the wrong gear, then fell over because their cadence was too slow, and they couldn't clip out of their pedals. She yelled at me about the hill. I didn't want that to be my first experience, so I played it safe and *walked* up the hill with my bike.

The forty-kilometer bike ride was flat—as my friend had told me—but it felt like riding one hundred miles. Coming into the transition was a relief, and as I racked my bike I also had a few more steps to complete than the other athletes—I had to change my biking leg into my running leg.

As I was running out of the transition area, I saw Elizabeth in the crowd. She yelled, "Great job, babe, but take off your bike helmet!" I smiled, jogged back, and placed my helmet with my gear.

The run was also flat, but I had to stop every mile to readjust my leg. It wasn't fitting quite right and I'd already developed a sore from the bike ride. The run proved to be very painful. Due to the heat and sweating, I couldn't keep the sleeve of my prosthetic dry, and that only added to the sting from the sore.

After a long, hot, 6.2 miles, coming across the finish line was an amazing feeling. I'd finished the race in two hours and thirty-eight minutes. For my first race, I had not only finished, but had done exceptionally well. I was officially *in love* with triathlons, and ever since that first race, I have only thought of ways to be more efficient and faster.

My first Half-Ironman distance triathlon was another learning experience. The swim was no problem. I had figured this thing out. On the bike at about mile thirty-five, feeling great, I reached down to grab my water bottle and took a drink. I went to replace the water bottle back into the cage, accidently bumped my release button on the inside of my cycling leg, and *off came my leg*. My leg was still rotating with the pedals and as soon as my leg hit the pavement, it catapulted me off my bike. I landed on my head, cracked my helmet, and my leg went into a ditch. It was on a turn, so volunteers were there to direct us around the corner. I remember one of the volunteer ladies screaming, "Oh my God, are you OK?"

I got up, did a quick inventory check, and asked the lady if she could help me find my leg. After a few minutes she found it and returned it to me. My leg was pointing in the wrong direction— out of alignment from the crash. I got out my Allen wrench, made some adjustments, and dusted myself off. I thanked the kind lady and told her that it was OK to laugh, it *was* quite a sight. She was horrified, but probably has a good story to tell her kids.

The next day, I went to the leg doctor and we made some adjustment to make the accidental leg release button *away* from my bottle cage.

The Ironman World Championship in Kona, Hawaii was my first Ironman distance triathlon. Physically-challenged athletes were picked from a lottery system. I was not sure I would get it, but I entered anyway. Next thing I knew, I was training for an Ironman. 140.6 miles did seem impossible. I didn't have a coach and really didn't have a clue. All I knew was I really loved a challenge and I wasn't afraid of the hard work. I bought a couple of triathlete magazines and an Ironman training book. *Ignorance is bliss.*

That morning, it was dark and I was terrified. I had never swum that far, much less in an ocean. Getting into the water, there was tons of nervous energy. *Where do I start in this organized mess?* The cannon went off and my heart was pounding out of my chest. I put my face in the water and swam like hell, hoping for the best. There were fish to look at—much different than the lane lines I was used to in the pool—but it was no leisurely ocean swim. If I slowed for one second, I got pummeled. About an hour and twenty minutes later, I was hopping up the steps, wondering if my leg was waiting for me. Thankfully, my handler was ready and waiting.

I was excited for the bike, because that was my favorite of the three sports. I had heard about the heat, wind, and humidity in Kona, and that took away my confidence going into it a bit. The bike was eye opening, to say the least. One hundred and twelve miles through Kailua, Kona was brutal. The heat and winds lived up to their reputation. I remember at mile one hundred being so excited to get off the bike. My butt was killing me!

As I was coming off the bike, I heard Mike Riley announce the winner of the race. That was *brutal.* When I got off the bike, I was destroyed. My legs felt like I was carrying rocks. However, my butt felt much better. *Positive thinking.*

In the transition area, I made my leg change and headed out for the 26.2 mile run. I had no idea how hard this event really was or what to expect my body to do. Thankfully, it held up and I finished the race in thirteen hours and nine minutes. Coming down the finishing shoot was a feeling like no other. All of my emotions of the whole day came to the surface when Mike Riley said, "Jeff Glasbrenner—*you* are an Ironman!"

Above: First triathlon, Memphis in May. Mechanical leg change.
Below: Ironman Malaysia

**Above: Ironman World Championships – Kona, Hawaii
Below: Hot Springs, AR triathlon. Photo: Jerry Dawson**

DAY 8: BEIJING TO HAWAII

"If I were asked to give what I consider the single most useful bit of advice for all humanity it would be this: Expect trouble as an inevitable part of life and when it comes, hold your head high, look it squarely in the eye and say, 'I will be bigger than you. You cannot defeat me.'"
– Ann Landers

The year 2008 was a busy one. I made my third Paralympic team and was also going to compete in the Ironman World championships. Those were the two biggest events on the schedule, but I also still competed on my Club team—the Dallas Mavericks—along with doing other triathlons.

The Paralympic team arrived in Beijing, China about a week before the Paralympics began. We made it to the Paralympics' village and got settled into our part. All of Team USA was put together in a section, so all the athletes representing our country stayed together in two different buildings. Six of us stayed together in a three-room suite sharing two bathrooms. The shower often times plugged up!

I brought my bike and bike trainer along with me so I could train for my Ironman. As a team, we normally had two practices a day along with film sessions. In between this time, we were free to do anything—roam the Paralympic village, watch video, rest, or whatever.

At the Village they had a twenty-four-hour cafeteria. The cafeteria had all different types of food, from salad to sushi to an all-you-can-eat McDonalds. The cafeteria was amazing. All the different countries' athletes came together to eat in one place. All the athletes wore their country gear, so one time you would sit down and eat next to someone from Russia, and the next it might be someone from Egypt. Add to that all the different disabilities, and it was a circus—visually impaired people, people in power or manual chairs, and a lot of amputees.

When we had free time from our team's activity, I trained for the triathlon. It was the perfect place to train. I had an Olympic size swimming pool, a big gym, and a lot of areas to run. Some days I would leave the Olympic village and go for a run in the city.

This is where I got to see a different side of China. It was much different than what they showed on TV. The places where I did my long run were polluted and impoverished. When I run, most of the time I forget that I am different, being an amputee. Running by many people, it was very evident that I was very different.

We learned that most of the time when a person has a disability in China they are pretty much locked up and forgotten about. I believe it was a nice byproduct of the games to let people of China see that people with disabilities can still do amazing things and become an active, productive member of society. I realized my running leg cost more than most of the houses I was running by. Often, I think we Americans forget the opportunities we have. I hear people worry about what is on TV tonight. The people I saw had *real* worries in their lives. They were dealing with what or how they were going to eat that day, or if they were going to have a roof over their heads. Never take your gifts for granted.

For opening ceremonies for the 2008 Games, we had one hundred and ten thousand people cheering us on as we entered the Bird's Nest. That was truly an amazing experience. The show they put on was just incredible. What the people at home don't see is that the athletes have to wait in a staging area for several hours before their country is called to march in. It was amazing, but also a long day and night. Some athletes or teams choose to skip the ceremonies, because of all the time and energy spent to be a part of it. I am happy to say we went and enjoyed the experience.

For some athletes at the games, they only have one event. They may have a qualifying round for the finals, then the finals, and their competitive time is over for the games. Then that athlete can relax, party, and just enjoy the games. Our team pretty much had to play every day.

We were the favorites for the Gold. We had three major competitions leading up to the games and had won them all.

We felt very confident. We played our pool B play and won all of our games, except one. We lost a surprising game to Great Britain—a team we had beaten every time before. I don't know if we just overlooked them or just had an off day.

We beat Australia—the eventual Gold Medal winner—in a close game. The top four teams from each pool crossover and play each other, and the winner advances. In our first game of crossovers we faced Iran. We warmed up in the practice gym, and we noticed that Team Iran was not on the other side of the curtain dividing the courts. We were told to enter the coliseum and go through our normal warm up. Team Iran forfeited the game. They boycotted our game, because the next game they would face Israel if they lost to us. We had to stay on the court for twenty minutes after they played our national anthem. I actually felt sorry for the athletes of Iran, because they didn't make the decision not to play us—their Government did. They were the ones to really lose out. It was a weird experience.

Our second crossover game was against Canada, a team we had played three times. We had beaten them all three times, but the games were close. We knew we were in for a battle.

We get off to a great start, leading by almost twelve points at one point in the game. Then in the second half they battled back. With fifteen seconds left in regulation, Team USA was up by three points when a teammate of mine got fouled going to the basket. The referee blew the whistle and we got two free throws. I know we were all thinking, *If we hit one or both of these shots the game is over and we have a chance to play for our gold medal.* My teammate got to the line and missed the first shot. *No problem; let's just make this second shot and game over.* My teammate got to the line and missed the shot. Team Canada got the long rebound, and their best player put up a three pointer at the buzzer.

The first overtime was more of the same back and forth. Then with the score tied and five seconds left on the clock, Team Canada fouled one of my teammates and the referee made the call. So again, we went to the foul line for two free throws. My teammate went to the foul line. We missed both shots. Again. The game went into double overtime.

We ended up losing in double overtime, and our team was completely devastated. The locker room was very silent. Some players said, "We will get them next time." Those of us who have been around awhile knew that opportunities like that one only came around a few times. We were so drained that we lost the Bronze medal game to Great Britain, eighty-five to seventy-seven. In between all the games, I was still training every day for my Ironman. I would ride my bike on the trainer in the afternoon and swim or run in the late evenings. It was a good Paralympics, but I was devastated that we didn't come home with the Gold medal. I knew then that I wanted to come back and try and win the Gold in 2012.

Two weeks later, I went to Kona Hawaii for the Ironman World Championships. A week after I got home from the Paralympics, I went to New York City for a visit to my new prosthetist. My running leg was giving me a lot of problems so I went in to get a new one made. They always say it is never a good idea to run a marathon on a new pair of shoes, so I knew getting and running on my new prosthetic running leg was going to be a bad idea, but I didn't have another choice.

We decided to take our daughter, Grace, with us to Kona in 2008. She was almost 3 at the time. Our son, Gavin got to stay home and get spoiled by Grams and Pops. My wife, daughter, and I arrived in Kona a couple days before the race. It was very hot and humid, as predicted. I had been training a lot, but mostly for basketball. I did great on the swim, getting out of the water in under one hour and thirteen minutes. The first half of the bike I did fine. The wind really picked up in the second half and I got caught in a big cross wind that blew my bike a bit sideways. I landed in a little hole in the side of the road. Two of the spokes on my front wheel broke. Then the wheel was rubbing on the brake, which made it hard to go anywhere. I waited along the side of the road for the mechanical van to appear. I was lucky and only had to wait about thirty minutes. They took my race wheel and gave me a wheel to use for the remainder of the race. I finished the bike portion in a much slower time—because of the extreme winds and wheel issue—but was very happy to be getting off my bike at Transition Two.

Now for the big unknown—how would this new leg feel? From my first step I knew it was going to be painful. I made it to the first mile and had to stop to check my leg. It was already bleeding. I made it to mile three and saw my wife and daughter. I really needed to see them at that moment. I was really struggling and in a lot of pain. I told her that it was going to be a long day. She smiled at me and said, "You can do this. We believe in you!" I gave them both a kiss and painfully took off again.

It started getting really hot, so I started dumping water over my head to help cool me down. It worked great for cooling me down, but it was terrible on my leg. The sleeve that I use to keep my leg attached to me acts like a suction system. It has to be dry or it will slide off. If it gets wet at all, it causes my stump to piston and slide off, or cause even more sores and bleeding. My leg and stump sock were completely soaked from my error of dumping ice water over my head. I had to start walking at mile six. Somewhere before that, I dropped the towel that I was carrying for drying off my stump.

As I started heading down back toward town, I saw my wife and daughter sitting just outside our hotel - a little past the 6.5 mile marker. I needed a towel, but no one had one. I took a quick look at Grace and began yelling for my wife, "I need her shirt!" Grace, like most 3 year olds, loved to walk around naked, so we quickly got the little shirt off of her and that became my new towel. One of my fondest memories of that race was sitting down to fix my leg drinking Gatorade with my baby girl. Grace lovingly leaned down and kissed "Stumpy". You see, my kids have made friends with my leg – nicknaming it "Stumpy". Stumpy is a part of our family and they always like to make sure Stumpy is feeling ok.

With the new shirt, I was able to dry off my sleeve and stump to make it not slip as much, making it more comfortable to run. The run was still pretty painful.

I was actually featured on the 2008 Ironman World Championship video. They followed my progress and filmed one of my painful pit stops, where I used Grace's little yellow shirt. As hard as that day was, it was the most amazing feeling crossing that finish line. The best part of it was to see my wife and Grace at the end.

2008 Paralympic Games – Beijing, China to 2008 Ironman World Championships – Kona, Hawaii.

Left: Ironman World Champion, Craig Alexander.
Right: Ironman World Champion, Chrissie Wellington

DAY 9: ILLNESSES

"A wise man should consider that health is the greatest of human blessings,
and learn how by his own thought to derive benefit from his illnesses."

–Hippocrates

Before Elizabeth and I got married, I told her very emphatically that I *didn't* want to have kids. I had four younger brothers and sisters, and I had already raised my kids. My life was about *me*, and it was going to stay that way—or so I thought at the time. Elizabeth had to make a hard decision, because she had always envisioned her life with kids, but she decided she would rather be with me than without me, and that kids weren't necessary for us to have a full life together.

I remember the day that this all changed for me. Elizabeth's brother had a baby, Ben. We went to the hospital to celebrate and meet our new, *big*, nephew. I held him and watched Elizabeth hold him...and something came over me. As we left the hospital that day filled with so much joy, I turned to Elizabeth and said, "We should do that!" She was quick to question me and make sure I knew what I was saying, but I *knew* I wanted to experience that with her.

It took us about eight months after Elizabeth went off the pill to get pregnant. We were so excited. However, after about six weeks, Elizabeth had a miscarriage. It was brutal. However, she was able to get pregnant again fairly quickly after that. While she was pregnant, our sister-in-law, Angela, was pregnant too. Their due dates were within a couple of months, and it was a fun, long-running joke about who was going to get the family name, Callie—Elizabeth's Great Grandmother's name.

At some point early in the pregnancy, I started calling our baby Grace. Don't ask me why, it just seemed to fit. This was before we even knew we were having a girl. Elizabeth kept telling me, "This is going to be a problem if it's a boy!" At the time we found out we were having a girl, it seemed wrong to call her anything *but* Grace. I think God knew what was in store for us and so we named her appropriately. Then, Angela found out she was having a boy, so no one took the name Callie...for the time being.

One thing I have learned is that you must find humor in some piece of this mess, or you will suffer, your marriage will suffer, and most importantly, your children will suffer.

This current rollercoaster started the day Elizabeth went into labor with Grace—December 12, 2005. I call it a rollercoaster, not because of the ups and downs, but because when you ride a rollercoaster, part of the time you are laughing, and part of the time you are scared out of your mind. Having Grace was one of the best days of my life, but what Grace had to endure over the first six years of her life is unconscionable.

When we were still seven and a half weeks out from her due date, Elizabeth began having contractions and bleeding. I called the doctor. Obviously our first thought was that she was having a miscarriage. By the time we got in, she was already four centimeters dilated. We were immediately admitted to the hospital—not our planned hospital—and they gave Grace steroids for her lung development, hoping we could stop the labor. They gave Elizabeth Demerol to calm her and to keep her from having more contractions. I sat next to her bed, holding her hand and rubbing her hair. All I could do at this point was be strong for her and trust the doctors would take care of all of us.

About an hour later—while we were talking with each other and her Dad—her water broke. I have never been so scared.

Grace was breech and we didn't have a choice at that point but to take her via C-Section. Elizabeth had never had surgery and was really scared. I, unfortunately, have had a lot of experience with surgery, so I was ready for it. Elizabeth's main fear was being awake and knowing they were going to cut her stomach open.

I attempted to remain calm and supportive. I remember sitting on her left side up by her face. She looked over and asked me if they had cut her yet, because she wanted to know that it wasn't going to hurt. I looked up over the sheet toward the doctor and came back down to her and said, "Oh, yes honey, they have cut you." At that point, my focus turned to hearing that sweet baby cry.

The next words that came out of the doctor's mouth were, "Wow, she's big." Then, she cried. That was the most beautiful sound ever. The nurses were laughing and kept saying, "Look at her breech legs!" Elizabeth couldn't see her and didn't know what they were talking about. I explained in detail that her body was in a V-shape, bent with her legs up and her feet on either side of her head, right on her ears. Every time they pushed her legs down, they would pop back up into a V. The nurses were laughing—which is a good thing! They assured us that her legs would "calm down" after being wrapped up and forced down for several days. They were right.

Grace was five pounds and one ounce. She didn't have to be on a ventilator. She was a strong girl the day she was born. Because she was born before thirty-six weeks, she didn't have the skill for suck and swallow. So she had to be bottle-fed and had to *learn* how to eat. This was the first in a long line of things to come that we as parents had to learn so we could teach and care for her.

The day they discharged us from the hospital was an extremely hard day. We had to go home without our baby. That is a horrible feeling. When you leave for the hospital to go have your baby, you usually have things ready—a crib, stuffed animals, going-home-from-the-hospital-outfits, etc. In our case, none of this mattered—she was staying. Coming home to an empty house and Elizabeth's empty belly was not comforting. Selfishly, we got a few days to let Elizabeth recover from her surgery. We were able to go see Grace three times a day for feedings.

We were lucky that Grace only had to be in the hospital ten days. It was Christmas and they let us go home on December twenty-third. The rules were that **no one** could handle or see Grace for a month—until her due date. She basically had no immune system and getting sick *would* kill her. So, we took her home and had Christmas—just the three of us. Our families and friends didn't completely understand, and some thought we were over reacting. Well, if a doctor tells you your kid might die, that's enough for me. We decided to go to the lake for a few days and rest in seclusion. On our drive, we saw a cow giving birth to a calf—poignant.

The first time we let someone else hold Grace terrified me. It was Elizabeth's brother. I wasn't terrified because it was Vance, I was terrified because if she got sick, it was *our* fault. The overwhelming responsibility of being a parent is something I wasn't prepared for, and to have a child that was immune-compromised to start off just added to my apprehension. But, as more people saw her, and after she made it through her first runny nose, we started to feel better.

The doctors told us that Grace would have a time period where she would be behind in development, because she was premature, but with hard work and therapy, she would catch up.

That is where Elizabeth and I kicked in. With my work ethic and Elizabeth's level of detail and planning, we were *undoubtedly* going to catch her up. We started with a local school/

therapy center. They were a fabulous group, and they got Grace crawling and walking over time. During that growth phase, she began banging her forehead on the ground when she was frustrated. Poor Grace crawled around for a long time with a constant bruise. Once she started walking, she stopped the head banging and began breathing rapidly through her nose periodically. Still thinking it was behavioral and not much to it, we put up with it, trying to stop her when we could. (Keep this in mind. It will be important later.)

We found out we were pregnant with our second child when Grace was about thirteen months old. We were so excited when we found out we were having a boy. Now we would have one of each.

At about eighteen months, Grace was finally walking, but still in a crib. There was still no talking at this point, but everyone said, "Don't worry, she is just delayed." We thought all we had to do was get her caught up in time for kindergarten. That was our goal. So, we started to teach her sign language. (Baby Einstein is genius, by the way.)

First we had to learn it and then teach her. Grace grew to know about thirty words in sign language. That was a huge breakthrough for our family, because we could finally communicate with her and she didn't get nearly as frustrated. At the two-year-old checkup, the pediatrician was concerned that she still wasn't showing signs of any talking.

Here comes therapy number two. We were referred to a different speech therapy group. A therapist came to our house three days a week for an hour. We did that for six or eight months with zero results. I do not fault the therapist, it just became apparent that something *wasn't* right. When Grace turned three the funding for home therapy ran out and she had to have the therapy through her preschool—therapy source number three. We decided not to do that and to explore other options. We took Grace to Arkansas Children's Hospital to have her tested with some department. It was there that we discovered that she had Apraxia.

Apraxia is characterized by loss of the ability to execute or carry out learned purposeful movements, despite having the desire and the physical ability to perform the movements. It is a disorder of motor planning, which may be acquired or developmental.

At this point we began to learn that the difference between a therapist's diagnoses and physician's diagnoses don't necessarily go hand in hand. I took that diagnosis back to the original school/therapy center—since we had good luck there—and they had a therapist who had been trained to teach kids with Apraxia. We got her going, ASAP, thanks to the school, and we had three training sessions.

At that point, I stopped it. Grace was being taught an entire new set of hand and body movements to go along with each word. She was extremely frustrated, and so was I. I still, to this day, don't understand why you wouldn't just teach sign language if movements were the method to use. I also learned, through that experience, that you don't waste time on something you know in your gut *isn't* right.

Several times after that, I wished I had remembered what I learned that day. At this point, we were at least eight or nine months into some sort of speech therapy, and we had nothing to show for it. Everyone kept saying, *she was premature, give her time,* but in my mind, our time to get her caught up for kindergarten was running out.

Gavin

On October 18, 2005, one of the other best days of my life happened. Our sweet, beautiful baby boy, Gavin, was born. He was three weeks early. I think Elizabeth's body is just not meant to keep babies full term. He had what the nurses lovingly called the "wimpy white boy syndrome." They had to give him oxygen and keep him in the NICU for several days to make sure he was stable. Overall, he was very healthy.

Again, though, we drove away from the hospital *without* our baby. This was devastating. Soon, Gavin was home, and we had a child we could share with our family and friends this time. At about three weeks old, Gavin started crying and wouldn't stop. If you have ever had a child, everyone you know has a remedy. We tried Karo syrup, suppositories, putting him on top of the dryer to make him rest, *everything*—and nothing worked. He cried non-stop and wasn't sleeping. Elizabeth was three weeks out of surgery, feeling better, but still tired and sore.

It came upon the week of Thanksgiving—Gavin was about four weeks old. My family arrived in town and we were set for a beautiful family holiday. The night before everyone arrived, Gavin *finally* fell asleep on the couch. Elizabeth announced that we were **not** going to touch him. This was the first time in about ten days that he had actually slept. About 9 p.m. that night—after two hours of sleeping—we heard him crying. Elizabeth went in to pick him up and he was burning with fever. She took his temperature and it was 103.7. We quickly pulled out the *What to Expect* book to see if we could give him Tylenol. We weren't sure, because of his age. In the book, it mentioned if your child is less than two months old with a fever over one hundred point two, to call the doctor immediately. Elizabeth did.

She got a call back from the nurse and asked if she could give our four week old baby Tylenol. The woman on the other end of the phone calmly, but sternly, said to her, "I don't want to scare you, but wrap that baby up and take him to the nearest emergency room *now*."

I giggled a little and thought to myself, *Whatever!* Elizabeth asked again if we couldn't just give him Tylenol to see if that helped. The nurse said no, and repeated her instructions. At that point, Elizabeth started to panic. I told her to do what she needed to do—typical male. So, she packed up Gavin and went to Children's Hospital. I stayed home with Grace, thinking that this whole thing was a complete overreaction.

Elizabeth Recounts Her Visit

At night there, you have to go through a metal detector. I came in and a very nice nurse stood up and said, "What is wrong with that baby?" I told her he had a high fever and she said, "Get that blanket off of him then and follow me." She opened the double doors of the Emergency Room and all I saw was people. People everywhere. Crying babies. I looked at her with a tear in my eye— I

was tired and still not one hundred percent from my surgery—
and said, "I can't do this." She quickly responded not to worry,
that we were taking Gavin back now. They gave him Tylenol right
away and took his temperature again—one hundred and three.
We were put in a room. A doctor came in fairly quickly and said
they needed to treat Gavin like he had everything, because if they
waited, it could be bad. At that point, I knew this wasn't good so
I called Jeff. My Dad went over to relieve Jeff and he came to the
hospital.

The plan was to start Gavin immediately on two types of
IV antibiotics, just in case. They feared an infection was running rampant in him. The next step was a spinal tap. The doctor explained that it was very hard to watch on a baby, because
of the way they had to hold him down. Elizabeth chose not to
watch. I told her, "I am not leaving him. I am staying." After a
few minutes of blood curdling screams from my brand new
baby boy, I had to leave. Elizabeth said my face was white as a
sheet, and all I could get out of my mouth was, "Where is the
bathroom?"

The doctor was right—not an easy thing to watch. Especially
when they had to stick him *twice,* because the first time they
missed.

About 1 a.m. Gavin was admitted to the hospital, and the
doctors said it would take over twenty-four hours to get the
labs back on the spinal culture. So, there we were, about to
spend Thanksgiving in the hospital.

After several days of tests confirming infection and meeting
with the infectious disease doctors, the doctor said to us, "If you

had waited even twenty-four hours to bring Gavin in, it could have been disastrous." Gavin had bacterial spinal meningitis. *Seriously, how does this happen?*

Many people have said to me since then, the good thing is that you got your "really bad thing" out of the way, but if you look at things as gifts, it actually turned out to be a good thing, because everything worked right for Gavin that night. The lady on the phone—who I consider Gavin's angel—Elizabeth's insistence to go ahead and take him to the hospital, the nurse at the entrance of the hospital, the doctors for starting treatment, and a lot of love and prayers from family and friends.

Gavin was given a PICC line (a peripherally inserted central catheter). It is a small tube that was inserted into his upper arm and terminates in a large vein in the chest near the heart. It was a way for us to give him antibiotics intravenously without having to stay in the hospital. We did several weeks of home antibiotics through a PICC line. Gavin slowly got better, and he has been healthy, happy, and growing ever since. We were lucky.

In January 2009, right about the time we started to freak out about Grace's progress—or lack thereof—a family friend of Elizabeth's called and said, "I am not your mother, but I insist that you go to Access Schools and meet with them about Grace and what they might be able to do for her." We were reluctant and were tired, but we were out of choices, so we went. This lesson taught me to keep fighting, because you never know when the tides will turn based on a decision you make. That meeting was enlightening and our decision to move Grace to Access Schools changed our lives forever.

As Grace began to make progress, we thought we were finally on our road to kindergarten. She began to talk and engage. It was amazing. Hearing her say "I love you" for the first time was indescribable, but in the fall of 2009, the teachers called Elizabeth one day at work and said Grace was having staring spells and episodes where her pupils went really small for a long period of time. We had never seen that at home, but at the advice of the school, we took her to a neurologist to see if they had any insight.

Our first visit to the neurologist was a scary one. Doctors tend to throw o t "what ifs." Elizabeth is a researcher and wanted to know hat it all was and meant. They scheduled Grace for a video EEG (Electroencenphalography)and said we might stay up to five days to try and catch a spell on tape. For an EEG test, multiple electrodes are glued to the patient's scalp and the EEG records voltage fluctuations in the brain. They were looking for seizures. Five days, and nothing, but the neurologist called Genetics to come see her while we were there.

The geneticist immediately noticed her skin pigment wasn't totally even on her arms, chest and legs. We thought that was just a side effect of her being premature and not fully developed. She was tested for several genetic disorders and we got a diagnosis—Mosaic Tetrosomy 5P.

This type of genetic disorder is extremely rare and only a few cases have even been documented in the *world*. Basically, Grace's cells were normal at conception, but somewhere along the split process, one cell split incorrectly, and she had two extra short arms of the fifth chromosome—hence the *5P*. After that one cell formed wrong, everything that split from that cell went wrong. Not all cells in her body are wrong—hence the *Mosaic*. The problem with this disorder is you are never really sure where the bad cells went. Clearly, some went to her skin, but we were now coming to believe that the rest went to her brain. The documented cases of this disorder didn't necessarily fit anything Grace was dealing with, but the doctors warned us of possible seizures and heart issues someday.

With not much else to go on, we went about our quest to "catch her up." In the summer of 2010, Grace began having issues after she woke up in the morning and from naps. She would hold her breath, stare, and then her head would drop violently. Although, it always appeared she was still *with us* and not really zoned out.

We consulted with a neurologist that specialized in Turrets, thinking it could be some sort of tick. She hooked Grace up again to the EEG—this time it was for eight hours. Elizabeth had video on her phone of Grace's episodes. After that EEG, the doctor said, "She doesn't have Turrets, she's having seizures." In a matter of ten minutes, our lives changed forever. The doctor promptly prescribed Keppra and said we needed to start it ASAP. We frantically began questioning and trying to understand and comprehend what she was telling us, but there was no discussion. This is what it was and this is what we were going to do.

The first time we put that pill in her mouth was devastating. We were giving our daughter something that was altering her brain. This was a Friday evening. Grace's episodes up until this point were head drops—scary but not overwhelming. After two days on the medication, Grace began falling with her episodes.

I remember the first time she fell. I thought, *Holy shit! What is happening?* The Sunday after we started the Keppra, we were sitting on our bed, Grace had one of her episodes, and instead of just dropping her head, she fell sideways—completely limp—in between the bed and the bedside table. She was hurt. On Monday morning, Elizabeth called the neurologist's office and was told that the doctor we had seen was off for a month and a half, and that because Grace was "her" patient we couldn't see anyone else. Our fear was that the medication was making her worse and we wanted to stop giving it to her.

Elizabeth asked what our options were for that day, and at 4:50 p.m. that afternoon, the nurse called back and said that our only option was to wait the month and a half for the doctor to return or take her to the emergency room. We chose the ER.

They admitted Grace that night to the hospital and hooked her up *again* to EEG. Luckily, another neurologist was on call that night and they said there is no way that the medicine was making her worse on the small dose she was taking. They ramped up the dosage. We were scared, but the doctors are supposed to know best. Right?

Over the next couple of months, they added a drug called Topomax. Grace continued to deteriorate. After about four weeks on Topomax, Grace could barely stand by herself. It was pitiful. In a matter of months our vibrant young girl—who was full of energy, but having weird head drops when she woke up—changed to a baby girl who was lethargic and falling about every five minutes. This was confusing and devastating. We called the neurologist and demanded that they take her off this medicine. It took six to eight weeks to get her off all of it.

She started to get a little better. Could there be a correlation? We were told **no** over and over again. The third medicine was started and stopped just as quickly, because she got worse again.

By February, it was decided to admit her for yet another EEG to see where we were. And yet *another* medicine came with it. And *again,* her symptoms worsened. The neurologist suggested that we try the Modified Atkins Diet to see if that would help. We were put in touch with a dietician at the hospital that made suggestions on how to do this, but really offered no real hands-on help with the process. She never met Grace face to face.

The goal was high fat and low carbs. Elizabeth researched and joined message boards for recipes. Our goal—according to the dietician—was high ketones on the urine stick with which we had to test her. We hit high ketones and no change. Grace began to not feel well, and it just wasn't working. Something wasn't right. We were so frustrated at this point and we felt like Grace was not getting the attention she deserved with her rare, dangerous condition.

We decided to pursue another hospital. Elizabeth made a lot of calls and came down to the possibility of going to the Mayo Clinic to see a true Epileptologist. A wonderful doctor there agreed to see Grace and we scheduled our first trip to Mayo.

When you go to a place like that, you begin to see what you envision your care *should* look like. That first trip was extremely hard for us—it is where we got the *true* picture of what was really going on with our baby.

Bring It!

On our first visit to the Mayo Clinic, they decided to do another EEG, which meant hooking her up to the head leads again for monitoring. Poor Grace had been through that several times now, so she knew what was coming. About half way through the process of gluing wires to her head, the male technician that was helping hold her down felt Grace give in a little and relax. He let up his hold on her and basically held her chin and talked to her. After they glue the wires on, they have to put gel in each of the nodes, and it scratches her head some when they do that initially. The first one they "gelled," Grace perked up and became strong again, fighting back. The male technician said, "Now she's going to bring her fight."

Grace immediately glared at him and said, "Bring it," in the sternest voice I have ever heard come out of a little girl— a moment of levity in all this madness. When we all started laughing, she laughed—not sure why, but she did. I love to see her laugh. She then proceeded to cry out for her brother. "I want my Gavin" is what she would say. Grace and Gavin have a special bond. We weren't sure how Gavin would take being at the hospital all this time being so young. We were lucky that my sister and her husband lived within an hour of Mayo Clinic. They came and got Gavin to stay with them for the time we were in the hospital. He got to play, learn to shoot his new kids bow and an arrow and get spoiled by his Aunt and Uncle.

The doctor came in to see us on the last day and said that Grace was one of the worst seizure cases she had seen. At this point, our baby was having seizures every two minutes—thirty seizures an hour—most of which caused her to drop to the floor. No wonder she wasn't progressing much in school. Her seizures were classified officially as multi-focal—meaning they were firing from all over her brain rather than coming from one place. Thus, she was not a candidate for brain surgery.

The doctor at Mayo validated that seizure medications make you worse on rare occasions and understood the implications of that. She also said that Grace was in *starvation ketosis*—her body was not getting the nutrients it needed. As parents, this was devastating—*we* were hurting our daughter on top of everything else. Elizabeth was so frustrated that it appeared she had a hard time keeping her emotions in. It was time for me to be strong and figure out the next steps.

The group all agreed that we would come back to Mayo Clinic and admit Grace to be placed on the Ketogenic diet. Although the diet didn't work for us, we had *finally* found a group that seemed to truly *want* Grace to get better. Besides, Elizabeth and this doctor were a lot alike in the way they thought and communicated— a great fit for everyone.

By summer, we were now at a point to decide if we wanted to start a heavy hitting medicine that could ultimately cause organ damage, but had good luck with this type of seizures. We decided to think on it, because we had a trip scheduled to northern Wisconsin with my family for a week. We thought it would be a good week to get some perspective on our next steps. That week was miserable for Grace. She was at her peak (or so we thought) with seizures. We had decided that we had to try the more dangerous medicines at this point. There was no way she could live a meaningful life in the state she was in at that time. But, how do you possibly choose to give your child a medication that could ultimately hurt her?

I am a big believer that everything happens for a reason. I believe that pretty much everything and everyone we encounter is by design. My accident—while horrible at the time—made me a better person. It opened my eyes to a different life. It made me do more with less. It gave me opportunities I never thought were possible.

Exactly one week after our trip, on a Sunday afternoon at the end of July 2011, we went to the ER at Children's hospital because Grace appeared to be having hallucinations mixed with her seizures. She was seeing spiders and other animals that scared her and gave her super human strength. She would look over her shoulder, or down at her legs, and freak out. It reminded us of a scary movie. She was going to hurt herself.

I was holding Grace on the floor of our living room with all of my strength. With tears in both our eyes, Elizabeth said, "What the hell is this?" Just when we thought it really couldn't be any worse for our baby girl...It was hard for us to protect her from herself, so we went to the ER to find answers. They found an abundance of abnormal brain waves on the EEG and immediately admitted us to the Pediatric Intensive Care Unit (PICU).

The doctors were puzzled to say the least. They didn't know why she was seeing things. Was it a virus? Did she eat something? Was it an infection? Or was it the next step or stage in her seizure activity? We finally got into the PICU hospital room around midnight. They gave Grace a sedative to relax her, but it didn't work. Grace is a fighter—she was still seeing her spiders. Then they gave her *another* sedative and our baby started resting peacefully. Elizabeth and I had bruises from holding our little girl while she was kicking those spiders away.

Grace had another MRI that day to check for swelling or anything abnormal. We stayed with her while they put the mask over her mouth to put her under. That was a sad and scary thing for me personally. Some people are afraid of heights—I am afraid of that mask they put over you when you have a surgery. It brings back so many memories of when I was in the hospital after my accident. I always felt like it was suffocating me and that I would die. It brought tears to my eyes for her.

After the MRI they did a spinal tap. Both of those procedures came back OK. The MRI was stable, as compared to her MRI a couple of months ago. During this time, Grace was off of all seizure medicine. With all of her seizure medication, it took a long time to get into her system before we knew if it worked. Then, once we discovered it didn't work, it took weeks to slowly come off the medication. During the course of the year, we had done this with five medications and the Ketogentic diet.

After all the regular testing came back negative, they agreed this was a new type of seizure coming to the surface. We saw yet *another* neurologist that was on call. He presented us with some choices and discussed with our Mayo Clinic doctor as well. Our choices were to start the high powered medicine with weekly blood tests or admit her to the regular hospital floor and try to accelerate some other less scary drugs through IV to see if we could see any improvement. He was extremely patient and helped us make the decision.

It wasn't likely any of these medications would work. But, what was another week if we could find a drug with fewer side effects that would help? In the hospital, we could take the seizure medications in a faster way through the IV or at a higher dose, because they could closely monitor Grace. They were able to take Grace's blood cultures hourly if needed to see if the medication was hurting Grace's organs or body. It took *weeks* to ramp up the medication when we gave it at home.

The first drug given to her via IV did nothing. She had an allergic reaction to the second. In the third medication, we found a glimmer of hope. It was a very old drug—Phenobarbital. She was extremely sleepy and loopy, but over a couple of days she seemed better. We were sent home on the medicine and we saw a lot of improvement in Grace's seizures. She went from thirty seizures an hour to about fifty seizures a day. We were so excited about it that we were afraid to talk about it, not wanting to jinx our good luck. Most people say we are crazy for feeling happy about fifty seizures a day, but where we had come from, it was *amazing*.

After three weeks on the drug, the very day after we increased her dosage of Phenobarbital, Grace started running high fevers. These weren't just little fevers–they spiked often to one hundred and four. We alternated Ibuprofen and Tylenol to try and keep the fevers down. Elizabeth called and asked the neurologist if it was possible the increase in medication could do this. And, as usual, we were told that it wasn't possible.

After three days of this fever, we took her to our local Primary Care Physician and were told Grace had strep throat. We were given an antibiotic and sent home. Two days later, she still had a high fever, and now she had a rash, so back to the doctor we went. They gave her a shot and sent us home on *another* antibiotic. Both times we explained the medicines she was taking and said the only change had been the Phenobarbital. We were told again that the drug didn't cause high fevers and the strep was causing the problem.

Three days later, we were back to the PCP with the same high fever. They bluntly said they had done about all they could do and they feared that she might have something called Kawasaki's disease. At this point she was starting to develop a really bad rash that looked like hives and no fever relief. They sent us on to the ER for more testing. We were admitted to Children's Hospital to attempt to reduce the fever and to find out what was causing her sickness. We asked again and were told it *wasn't* the Phenobarbital. They did testing on all different illnesses. All the names they were throwing out about what it could be were very scary—Google is not always the bearer of good news or information. The Infectious Disease doctor on call that night suspected she did have Kawasaki's, but there was no real test for it.

The next day, we were lucky enough that the head neurologist was on call. He said that it most definitely *could* be a reaction to the Phenobarbital. This is what we thought the whole time—after all, Mother knows best. The problem was and always is that Grace doesn't play by the rules. With all of these illnesses they were talking about, she didn't fit into any one of them perfectly. She had four or five of the major symptoms, but never all of them.

The doctors felt they had to treat her for Kawasaki's disease, just in case, because if left untreated it could lead to death. So they gave her a dose of IVIG—blood plasma from twenty thousand people. This was a very expensive IV treatment—about ten thousand dollars a dose. She had two doses. It appeared things were spiraling a bit out of control. Her blood levels were all out of whack – she required blood transfusions. At the same time, we stopped the Phenobarbital, but the half-life of that medication is long and so it was going to take days to fully get out of her system. Her rash got worse and her fever didn't subside. Over several days, they decided to start a course of steroids, because if the fever and rash was a reaction to the Phenobarbital, it was called DRESS syndrome. This is a severe drug reaction that usually comes on three to six weeks after starting certain drugs—Phenobarbital being one of those drugs. But, starting steroids would weaken her immune system.

The rash began to get a little better and seemed to be running its course, but the fever never really subsided. After about a week, she seemed to feel better. Then, as quick as she got better, she started declining again. Over the next ten days she was poked and prodded way too much. They had taken a lot of blood for testing and her little veins were not doing well. Her kidneys started showing signs of problems. Her blood counts weren't recovering. The rash started over. Things weren't good.

They decided to get Grace a PICC line so they could draw blood without having to poke her each time. This was a temporary line that started in your upper arm and ran toward your heart. They took her down to put in the PICC line and all seemed normal. We were grateful that they wouldn't have to wake her up each morning with blood draws. While her condition seemed to be worsening, the most encouraging thing was, she stopped having seizures—completely. Something had happened, but no one was really sure *what*. We just didn't talk about it.

That night after receiving the PICC, Grace began to complain that her arm hurt. It was infected. She was deteriorating again, and fast. She was scheduled for an MRI one afternoon on her arm to see if they could tell how bad the infection was. By that afternoon, Grace's fever was one hundred and six and uncontrolled. She was on ice blankets. It was not good. Her heart rate was holding steady at two hundred beats per minute. Finally, something I understood. Being an athlete, you are trained to know when your heart rate is too high. Two hundred beats per minute was extremely high. The physician's team quickly moved her to PICU to be monitored more closely. They bombarded her with rapid infused fluids, she needed blood transfusions, and her platelet count was dropping. She was going to need those too. Once stable, they took her to MRI to look at her arm and the PICC line itself.

We got to go with Grace down to the MRI room, but only so far, because of my artificial leg. An MRI Machine is one big magnet. Let your imagination soar about how funny that would be if I got too close. About two hours later, they wheeled her back into the PICU room and she was sedated and on a ventilator. The anesthesiologist told us that Grace did really well. My response: "Why are you breathing for her then?" Grace's infection and her sepsis proved too much for her little body. Elizabeth lost it. "How is it possible that we came in with a high fever and now she might die?" That is by far the hardest thing to see—your child may not be able to breathe on her own. Luckily, there were some amazing doctors and nurses around that took the time to explain what we were seeing. They actually cared about us. We had a lot of hugs and prayers from those doctors and nurses. So many we could never repay them.

We were now two weeks into our hospital stay, tired, scared, and now not sure if Grace would live. The questions and comments we started getting from the doctors changed in focus— Do you want a private room in the waiting room? How is your support system in Little Rock? We are behind the eight-ball and now we need to play catch up. While honest and necessary, it's not easy to hear that your daughter might not make it through the night. I wondered if my Mom felt this way when I was in the hospital.

Grace had contracted a MRSA infection in the hospital from her infected PICC line. The line had to come out and it was decided she would need a central line in her neck. The ICU doctor kept telling us that she needed "more access" to Grace. As I've said, things were not good.

Grace remained intubated for the next two days. All of her blood counts were way out of control in a bad way. We were told she would probably be intubated for the next few days. Elizabeth and I had started trading off going home with Gavin every other night to spend time with him and to get some sleep. My sisters also flew in from Wisconsin to be with us. They knew what it was like to be in Gavin's shoes, to be shuffled all around to the different relatives and babysitters while a sibling was in the hospital. They wanted to spoil him and keep him busy.

It was Elizabeth's night to stay with Grace. That next morning, she proudly recounted the stories of the night to me. At midnight, Grace woke up out of sedation and tried to pull her breathing tube out. This was bad, because her throat and tongue were swollen, and the staff feared if it came out that they couldn't get it back in. They tried for two hours to sedate her to calm her down again. It took six adults to hold the little forty-pound girl down to keep her from hurting herself – one at her head, one on each limb and one holding the breathing tube in place. They kept hooking up more medicines to her central line to attempt to relax her.

After an hour of struggling, the doctor turned to my wife and said, "We have given her enough meds to put down a horse." It took still another hour to get her settled. That is when she became lovingly known as *the Warrior Princess* to everyone who came to talk with us.

That morning they decided Grace was strong enough to come off the breathing tube. That was monumental! She was now awake, getting better and still no seizures.

The next day on my usual coffee run down stairs, I exited the PICU area and went to the space to wash my hands – in the PICU you must wash your hands to enter and exit—and someone said, "Jeff Glasbrenner!" I turned and saw a young man. He said, "You probably don't remember me, but I used to referee some of your wheelchair basketball games." He went on to tell me that he was at the hospital with his son. They live in Rogers, Arkansas—about three hours northwest of Little Rock—and their son was running a fever and had become septic. His condition changed rapidly, and they had to be med-flighted to Arkansas Children's Hospital. The previous night, he had called my old coach at University of Whitewater to get my information, because he remembered I lived in Little Rock. He feared he would need my advice.

Doug told me all about his three-year old son's condition. Six beds down from my daughter's, he was also on a breathing tube and not doing great with sepsis. The doctors told Doug that his son's outer extremities were at risk for amputation. We exchanged our scary real life nightmares and went on our way. I was feeling very weird about how our paths had crossed. *Everything happens for a reason.*

The next day Doug's family received some good news after the doctor unwrapped the bandages on his son's legs. They were told that at the next day's surgery they would only have to remove the toes. Everyone, including me, was extremely happy about that. About two hours into the surgery, they were told they would have to remove both legs right below the knee. The family was devastated. I was too. I knew what this little guy would have to go through in life. I told the family that we would help in any way we could. Doug had so many questions. I hoped to be a resource for him and his family. I had so much help, and I hoped I could be that for Doug and his son.

The gift, you might wonder, was while Grace was in the hospital, her seizures stopped. We, and the doctors, have no idea why. We had gone from thirty seizures an hour to nothing. Everyone has a theory. Did the trauma rearrange something in her brain? Was it the IVIG treatment? Was it not eating for so long? Was it just a miracle? We don't know and may never know. I can tell you, though, I am proud to be the daddy of that little miracle. We live every day in amazement of the path Grace went down to end up here. We also live every day in fear of it coming back. But this is a gift, and we are going to recognize it as that. We may be faced with another gift later on, but for now, this is the best gift ever.

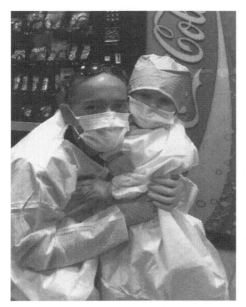

Above: My sister, Jenelle, entertaining Gavin while Grace was hospitalized.

Grace's first helmet.

Right: Grace and Gavin finding fun during one of many EEG tests in the hospital.

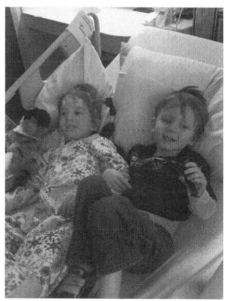

DAY 10: NOT FINISHING IRONMAN LOUISVILLE, KY

*"Defeat may serve as well as victory
to shake the soul and let the glory out."*
−Edwin Markham

It's hard to suffer. Even though you want to do away with the pain, you have this gut-wrenching feeling that you simply have to let it be. Deep down, you understand that you're a part of the formation of something infinitely bigger than if the pain were spared. You're beholding a stained glass portrait being pieced together in the darkest of hours, trusting the bleeding hand that places the broken shards side by side, and realizing that one day, when the light shines through, it will radiate with an unparalleled brilliance.

But it's difficult to believe it's beautiful while still in the dark. We were driving home to Little Rock, Arkansas from Louisville, Kentucky in my Yukon, full of sweaty triathlon clothing, disc wheels, carbon fiber bikes, and Burger King wrappers. The day before was the day that was probably one of the most challenging of my life. This was the day I cracked. I had arrived in Louisville confident, strong, and sure of myself and what I had to do. I returned to Little Rock broken, disappointed, and burdened.

Louisville was just another Ironman competition in my lineup for the "8-in-8" year. People tell me that I make an Ironman look easy, even though I am missing my right leg below the knee. This was the year I had set out to complete eight Ironman competitions in eight months to commemorate the thirtieth anniversary of losing my leg as an eight-year-old boy. I choose to never do anything in moderation—makes life more interesting. Louisville was number four of eight, and the totally unexpected happened—I was forced to quit due to severe dehydration. I had never quit anything I had set out to achieve. It went against everything in me, but my body simply shut down. I sometimes wonder if I'd had a choice, but it wasn't my day.

When I went to the emergency clinic, I looked horrible. I was shivering, my arms were full of tubes and a needle. Radiation blankets were bundled around me to warm me and were crackling as I moved in pain. Even though I was out of it for the most part, I was mostly hurting from my severe disappointment. My friends with me were clearly hurting for me as well. I was cramping and convulsing with cold chills. Through trembling lips, all I mumbled was, "I can't believe I didn't finish." The IV dripping vital nutrients into my body felt more like cold lead running through my veins. To be lying in that bed meant **I'd failed.**

My inability to accept defeat is often overwhelming. If someone doesn't believe in me, I will prove them wrong. There were a lot of people that didn't think I could do eight Ironmans in eight months. Now, for the first time in my life, I feared they were right. I am a fighter who has gleaned my life lessons from adversity, and I simply don't have the patience to put up with people who have no desire for growth. So, for me to quit shocked me more than anyone else.

After the medical team rehydrated me the shivering began to subside and I became more alert. My friends got my wife, Elizabeth, on the phone to assure her I was OK. She wasn't able to attend this particular race because of work.

The swim portion had been perfect. I completed four thousand meters down the Ohio River at a pace consistent with my other Ironman competitions. Clipping my biking leg into the pedal, I was in great position and felt strong. My demeanor was good—happy and confident coming out of the transition areas. I was determined.

Louisville is a rolling course, and it was a typical August Kentucky day—hot and fairly humid. With forty miles left to go in the one hundred and twelve mile bike course, I passed an aide station that had run out of water. All I had with me on the bike at this point was Infinit Nutrition mix for quick energy, so I was forced to take the only thing the aide station had to offer—Powerade. More sugar.

When I arrived at the following aide station, they were also out of water. At this point, I panicked. Desperate for anything, I once again filled up on Powerade and drank what I could.

The problem is, despite its electrolytes, this drink is full of simple carbohydrates that work best when diluted or taken with water...but there was no water. On top of that, I wasn't used to drinking Powerade along with my sponsored sports drink, Infinit Nutrition.

I rode the last forty miles without receiving any refills on water, and by the time I started the run, it was too late. I was severely dehydrated and had an upset stomach from all the sugar. With the high temperatures of Louisville that day, I had already lost an incredible amount of water and vital electrolytes through my sweat. My body's pH balance began to change chemically.

When the body is dehydrated, it becomes incredibly faint and extremely sensitive to chemical imbalances. The body ceases to sweat to try and preserve its mineral salts, which are necessary for cellular function. When the body doesn't sweat, it cannot cool itself—the temperature rises and the body goes into a feverish attempt to shut down any effort to continue. Cramping is usually the result.

I pushed through this miserable condition for hours. I tried to jog. I tried to walk. I tried sitting and resting. I tried "re-booting" my leg—that is what I call it when I wipe the sweat out of my leg liner. Sometimes giving my leg a breather helps. Because I was walking more than running, the height and springiness of the running leg—which is solely made for running—were irritating my leg. It's built based on my usual race pace to keep everything in line. I was far from that pace today. I even had my friend bring my other carbon fiber walking leg so I could try and just get to the finish line with less discomfort.

My friends brought me water to drink to attempt to replace what I had lost on the bike, but it was too late. I only made it a half-mile before I had to start walking, and I was puking by mile three. I forced my way to mile eighteen with sheer determination, but my body simply wouldn't allow me to continue. I collapsed at mile eighteen. An ambulance had to be alerted and I was rushed to the medical clinic. As the ambulance picked me up, I called my wife who was at a work-related dinner. I asked her to call my friends who were in Louisville because I couldn't remember their numbers and tell them I was being picked up by an ambulance. That was all I had the energy to do. Needless to say, I effectively worried my wife. Not good.

I am not about any excuses—I should have planned better. There must have been something I could have done to finish. Now all I have to show is a big DNF—DID NOT FINISH. I was so bitterly disappointed to be recovering on that hospital bed instead of at the finish line. In life, you can't rely on other people to always pick you up. You have to take care of yourself. Even though people want to help you, they won't always be at the right place at the right time. I am reminded of a funny story about people wanting to help and it just not working out:

Picture this. My son, Gavin—the spitting image of me— three-years-old going on twenty. Small build, extremely cute, and loves his five-year-old sister, Grace, more than Star Wars **and** pirates.

Grace was sitting on the edge of our bed one evening. Suddenly, she held her breath and Gavin said, "I got her Mom." This was a normal reaction in our house, because of Grace's rare seizure condition. "I got her" was our way of communicating when Grace was about to have a seizure and who would catch her to break her fall. So, Gavin took his stance in front of her next to the bed—knees bent and his arms up ready to catch her if she fell—sumo style. He looked like he was a quarterback about to take the snap. About the time Elizabeth and I made it into the room, Grace seized and fell sideways—not toward Gavin—and tumbled onto the carpet floor. Gavin stood straight up and said, "Well shit! Sorry, Dad!" He did not learn that word from me...

At that point, there was nothing to do but laugh. Grace perked up and said, "I'm OK." Moral of the story: you can have the most loving, supportive people around you to help, but ultimately, it's you that has to get up and be "OK."

It's a strange trait in human nature to second-guess oneself. Everyone does it on some level—whether it's a failed test, a failed relationship, or an unfinished race. You try and think about every possible way you could have done it differently or better. You think through your entire day, what you could have changed, and the factors you possibly could have controlled, but didn't when it mattered. The hardest challenge is just to let it go. To this day, I still have a hard time admitting I failed at that race. Even though no one else would ever say so, for the first time, I saw myself as a quitter.

I was thankful to have my friends there though. They got me back to the hotel and situated in bed, and then went back to collect all my equipment. The Ironman is a feat in and of itself for anyone, but a guy with one leg? I had a lot of equipment—a bike leg, a running leg, and a walking leg, in addition to goggles, a swim cap, a wetsuit, a bike, a helmet, cycling shoes, running shoes, nutrition, towels, and skin lubricant. You name it, I had it. So much time, so much effort, so much preparation, and I sat in the hotel room and felt it was all for nothing.

The following morning, I felt better. I was refreshed with a night of hard sleep. I joked about hosting a "DNF Party" once we got back to Little Rock, and we all laughed for a bit. You see, one thing you cannot do is dwell on something that is done. You have to put that in the past and move forward. Some people say, "Get back on the horse." I say, "Get back positive thinking and look forward." I think back to the gift I was supposed to take from that day. It was hard to recognize, but I gained an understanding of what a lot of people deal with in their lives— failure. The only difference in me is that my failure fueled me to not ever let it happen again.

Packing up the car with all the equipment and four bodies was a feat. We were all tired and ready to get home. Nine hours of highway were all that separated me from home, comfort, rest, my wife, Grace, and Gavin. As we started along the highway, we had tunes playing, and what else could we do but smile and make the best of the situation? I, of course, was still feeling the lingering sting of yesterday's defeat, but continued to crack jokes. Sometimes, laughter really is the best medicine.

We even decided fast food was in order. I don't have the best record of nutritional perfection, but I had been pretty dedicated to being healthy for this year of racing. Burger King was the destination of choice, and you'd think we had all descended upon the most delicious seven-course meal anyone had ever seen. It was ridiculous how much we all were enjoying the all-American deliciousness we'd denied ourselves for months.

In the middle of our feast in the car and great conversation, my buddy's phone rang. It was Elizabeth. She told him she had been trying to call my phone but couldn't get me. I was driving at that time. When I saw on the caller ID that it was Elizabeth, I was excited to hear from her and answered with a smile and a chipper hello. And then, silence.

Here's how my side of the conversation went. "Oh God...I can't believe this happened right now...have you talked to mom...oh no... I'll call my sisters...Do they know yet? OK...I love you, too. I'll call you soon." I hung up the phone. My face was on fire and my eyes got watery. I am not a big crier and I attempted to choke back the tears, but they began to fall. Exactly thirty years and thirty days after the horrible farming catastrophe that claimed my leg, I received word that my own father had passed away that afternoon in another farming accident.

DAY 11: PASSING OF MY FATHER

'Ohana' means family—no one gets left behind,
and no one is ever forgotten.
–Lilo & Stitch

My dad was a very hard individual. He didn't like mistakes and didn't accept not trying. He has really helped me become what I have become and helped me know what I don't want to become. He made me stronger, giving me a no-excuses-attitude. He taught me never to give up and never to feel sorry for myself. He told me I would *always* have to work harder than everyone else, because of my leg.

I remember shortly after losing my leg. I still had to use crutches to get around. The library at my school was located on the second floor. My dad found out that I had been missing out on library activity because it was on the second floor. He decided that wasn't an option.

I was very weak still and not able to go up all of those stairs, so the teacher just put me in the principal's office while she took the rest of the kids up to library class. My dad came into the principal's office and demanded something be done about getting me upstairs with my class. He made his point very clear that I wasn't going to miss my next library class, and made it clear that the principal would personally carry me up the flight of steps to class.

My Dad pushed all of us. My sister, Jenelle, was the best athlete in school, male or female. She was a superstar. I remember going to all of her games. She could score thirty points and my Dad would ask her why she missed the few shots she missed. When I started playing wheelchair basketball, I was sure to give it one hundred percent for fear of cuts from dad about not being the best.

Dad always pushed us. He was hard-core with me. He pushed me that I had to be better than average, that because I was disabled, I had to be twice as accurate, and twice as careful. He didn't allow screw-ups. It was a double-edged sword—it drove me to be good, but it was a lot of pressure as a kid.

My Mom, more so than Dad, came to my basketball games. She has been to the Paralympic Games in Athens, attended tournaments in the Netherlands, and in Spain. Dad didn't like to travel much. He would go to Las Vegas and Colorado, but wouldn't go abroad. However, he was always interested in whether I won and if *I* scored the most points.

Soon after my dreams of re-joining the national team were becoming a reality, my Dad was diagnosed with lung Cancer and was only given five months to live. I thought it over for a long while and decided to make a phone call to the USA Basketball Coach. I told him that I really wanted to be part of his National team, but just found out some bad news. I decided rather than being away and missing out on the time I could be with my dad and family, I decided not to try out for the team. This was the World Championship team—every other two years from the Paralympics.

I had already won two Gold medals in that competition. I felt like I had been there and done that, so it was much more important to stay close to home. In March of that year, the Rolling Razorbacks had a tournament in Las Vegas, Nevada. This was a tournament my parents never missed. They loved to gamble, and to watch me play. I knew it would be the last time my dad would probably get to see me play wheelchair basketball. I had a great tournament. In the last game, I went off scoring fifty points and taking over the game. My dad really enjoyed that—he was all smiles. After and between the games he slept and rested. The cancer was really starting to take over.

In June, I took my dad on a bucket-list trip to Colorado. As a kid, my Dad always took us to Colorado every year for family vacation. We usually went to the same places, and we all loved it. So, I decided it would be a great last trip for us. I got him a plane ticket from Madison to Denver and I drove my truck out to meet him at the airport.

I made the thirteen-hour drive, no problem. We did all of our usual haunts, like Mt. Evans, Royal Gorge, Cripple Creek, Central City and some Denver stores we had always visited.

I never like to be away from training too long, so I brought my running leg, cycling leg and bike with me to Colorado. One afternoon, I wanted to do some mountain climbing on the bike, so dad and I went to the bottom of the mountain that led up to Mount Evans. We stopped and got Dad a couple of news-papers—he loves to read the newspapers. We talked it over. I would go on an hour and a half ride while he read the paper to find us something fun and interesting to do that afternoon. He was to wait at the park and rest until I finished the ride.

With all of the medicine he had to take, he fell asleep all the time. We would be in the truck and in mid-sentence would nod off for a couple of minutes. So, driving was not a good option. I made it very clear to him that I didn't want him driving unless absolutely necessary, and he said OK!

It was an amazing bike ride up the mountain. In Arkansas, we don't have challenging mountain passes to ride every day. I really enjoyed the view and the challenge of making it up the mountain. I made it up to the top and turned around with the long descent back toward Dad. I made it back to the park and ride where Dad was stationed and I discovered the truck was missing. I started to panic. My ride had only taken me one hour and fifteen minutes. I was back in plenty of time for my hour and a half planned ride. Dad didn't have a cell phone and my cell phone didn't work in the mountains.

I had few options—no money, no phone, only my cycling outfit on, and it was really cold, and I only had my cycling leg, so I really couldn't walk anywhere—my cycling leg is very uncomfortable to walk even a few feet. My only option was to sit and wait it out.

One hour later, Dad showed up. He said he fell asleep and lost track of time, so he went up the hill to find me. Dad has always only followed his rules. He did things his way! I was panicked and pissed. He was not to drive, because it was dangerous, and he had left me stranded and worried.

In Dad's more mature years he really enjoyed playing slots at the casino. We made our base for the week in Black Hawk/Central City with a lot of gaming close by. It was amazing to watch how much fun someone could have playing penny slots... especially someone who usually only bet a penny a pull. I sat by his side for hours and talked about random things. At the end of the day, he would usually be up fifty bucks or so, but more importantly, he was smiling and having a blast. I am not much for gambling, I am way too competitive for that.

We went to restaurants that we normally would on our family trips, like Casa Bonita and the Black-Eyed Pea. We had a great time. On this trip, I also wanted to talk about my accident. I really wanted to just talk openly about it—what he was feeling and thinking when it happened, how he dealt with it, if he blamed himself.

Now, being a father myself, I can't imagine what he felt. I blame myself when my kiddos skin a knee. I wanted to talk about the accident for the *both* of us. I wanted him to get anything off his chest he wanted too. I asked him about that day, and he did his usual when I brought up the subject—change it, *fast!* I pried a little more, and the only thing he told me was that he knew I had to go through a lot, but I had made the best of it and he was so proud of me. He told me he thought that sometimes, bad things happened to good people, then he drifted off to sleep. He was from the era where men didn't talk about their feelings.

I didn't know what I was looking for, but that is what I got. I don't know if I was looking for *I'm sorry,* or *You shouldn't have been on that tractor with me.* After all, it was an accident. He didn't plan for it to happen. I never brought up the subject again.

He pretty much slept all that day, because of the medicine, and because he was growing weaker. The last day of the trip we went to a Colorado Rockies games. He liked baseball and I liked seeing him happy. We got good tickets and had a great time. We got a great picture together at the entrance of the ballpark. Giving up the opportunity to play on the national team was so worth that photo. I will never forget that moment.

In mid-July, my youngest sister moved her wedding date up to be able to have my Dad walk her down the aisle. The wedding took place in Negril, Jamaica. It was a small, but lively, destination wedding. It was great to have almost all of my brothers and sisters together—however, we missed my youngest brother and his family. It was priceless to see Dad walk my sister down the aisle—or rather, beach. He was so happy and so proud.

Thirty years and thirty days from the day that I lost my leg, my father passed away. Not from his lung cancer or diabetes, but from a tractor accident.

He was up on the hill pulling logs a couple of miles from the farm. There was a young kid with him that helped him out some on the farm. The ground was wet and muddy from the previous day's rain. My dad was in bad health, but he was bound and determined to *still* work on the farm. That was his life. He didn't quit, no matter how frail or unsteady he got.

The tractor wheel lost footing and the logs began to slide down the hill. The tractor was pulled over, threw him off, and rolled over him. He was dead right then. I reflect sometimes on how ironic it was that he passed away in a tractor accident—given all of our history—but he loved tractors and farming. It's comforting that he died doing something he loved and not in a nursing home suffering from lung cancer.

My father hardly ever told me he loved me, but I know he did. He rarely told me he was proud of me, but I heard that from him on our last bucket list trip, and from a lot of people at his funeral. Many told me how proud of me he was.

I hope I can impart some of his work ethic to my children. However, I *will* tell my children I love them *every day,* because I love them so much. I'm going to let my kids be the way they want to be. I'll force them to *try* and give them an opportunity to be surrounded by every possibility to find what they truly love, but not with that same pressure.

DAY 12: GIVING UP THE PARALYMPIC GOLD MEDAL

"To thine own self be true."
–William Shakespeare

When does going for the Gold cost too much?

Ever since my first day of playing wheelchair basketball, my goal or dream was to win a gold medal at the Paralympics. I have gone to three Paralympics and come home with the Bronze, seventh and fourth place. This is a long way from what I had wanted, so after the 2008 Paralympic Games in Beijing, I knew that I wanted to give it *one* more try to make that gold medal happen.

The Arkansas Rolling Razorbacks decided not to play the season before the Paralympic Games, because of an injury to a key player. They decided we wouldn't be in contention to win, so why even try? This was not my way of thinking or living. We decided to part ways shortly after that. This put me at a real disadvantage with my training for the US Tryouts.

It is hard to train for a team sport if you don't have a team or someone to train with. After my last 8-in-8 Ironman in December, I decided to switch my focus to training for wheelchair basketball. With an Ironman, you need to be lean and mean—eating is cheating. In wheelchair basketball, I needed size and bulk to be at my peak. I started focusing on gaining weight by lifting weights and focusing on nutrition—the fact that I wasn't running, biking, and swimming in volumes helped greatly with the weight gain. I trained really hard to get back into basketball shape, doing all the individual drills and shooting drills to gain my edge. However, it is very hard to train on your own.

Going into tryouts, I hadn't played against someone in almost a year. I knew I was going to be off some with timing on picks, defense, and shooting. I showed up to the Philadelphia tryouts mentally and physically ready to take on the challenge. Since my last tryouts, I had gained fifteen pounds.

The first day we had mostly timing drills and shooting drills. I knew I would do well with these, because that is something I trained everyday by myself. The second and third sessions of the day were five-on-five scrimmage. I was a bit nervous for the first scrimmage, because this is something I didn't have a chance to train for. I got a little rust off the first scrimmage and played well the rest of the tryouts. It had come back like I hoped it would. I left the tryouts feeling good about my chances of making the team and having that chance of going for the gold.

This year, the tryouts were run very differently than in the past. Everyone who wanted to try out had to send in a resume and letter from his coach, as well as video of him playing. In the past, tryouts were done by the coach and some committee members. Everyone invited attended the tryouts, and at the end of the four days the team was named. This time around, with the new coaches, they decided to give more people the opportunity to try out. Like most things in life, it can get political. This new tryouts system allowed *more* people the opportunity.

The new tryouts were also spread out over four different tryout camps instead of one. Each of the tryouts had about twenty-five people with different classifications. The camps were spread out over two months. After the last camp, the coaches selected eighteen athletes to be part of Team USA. In the past, twelve athletes were selected, with an additional three alternates if an injury or something occurred.

I was happy with the way that I played at my tryouts, but I didn't have a clue on how anyone at the other camps played. I decided not to worry about something I couldn't control. After the last tryout camp, I received a call from the coaches saying that I made the team of eighteen. I was extremely happy and excited. All eighteen members that were selected were considered on the team, up until the final tryouts a couple months before the 2012 Paralympics.

During the summer when Grace took a turn for the worse, our first team camp was in Chicago. Grace had not been doing well, so I really didn't want to go, but I went anyway. At the point of my leaving for that trip, she was peaking with the number of seizures she was having. It is so hard to watch your baby go through that. I wished I could just take all the bad away, even if that meant taking on the seizures myself, I wished for it. After the first training session, I got a call from Elizabeth and learned that Grace was taken to the emergency room.

Elizabeth and I had a deal—she was to always tell me the truth about how our family was when I was away. She never wanted to worry me, but I needed to know. Grace had been given a new seizure drug and it was making her throw up and have diarrhea. It is so hard to practice and play a *game* when you know your little one is suffering. I felt for my wife, because not only did she have to worry about Grace falling off the toilet from a seizure, but now she had vomiting and diarrhea to contend with *while* holding her up.

I had an OK camp, but was really not into it. My thoughts and energy were still focused back home. I was the second oldest player on the team. When I first started playing on the national team, I was one of the youngest. Now I was competing against guys that were twenty years younger than I am. They are talking about all of the girls they are going to get, and all I could think about was my little Grace. To say we were in different places in life was an understatement. On the national team, we had a lot of team training camps and competitions. Many of the team's training camps lasted a week. Most months, we got together twice, so that was a lot of time away, not to mention all of the *individual* training.

Just before the end of the July competition in Toronto, Canada, Grace's condition was worsening. She was still having over thirty seizures an hour and was continuing to fall down and hurt herself. She wore a pink helmet around *all the time* to help protect her from the falls. During this time, we pretty much had to be by her side to protect her. Every one and a half to two minutes we needed to be next to her. We had to start removing furniture from the house, because it was dangerous. We took her bed out of her room and put the mattress on the floor. Grace has never been a good sleeper and she got up a lot in the middle of the night. She would have seizures when she got up and fall out of bed. We removed the coffee table in the living room, because she liked to sit by it but would have a seizure and hit her head on the corner. We couldn't eat at the supper table, because she would have seizures and hit her face and legs on the table, often falling out of her chair onto our hardwood floor, so we ate Japanese style on the floor, as a family, because it was safer for Grace. It was tough to explain to Gavin why we moved our furniture and why we had to eat picnic style, but he got it.

One day—before we decided to stop eating at the table altogether—we thought about "padding" the table. So, I took Gavin to Home Depot to try and buy some padding we could secure to the table. I explained to him that we needed to help protect Grace from hurting herself. He liked being a part of keeping her safe. We went home and fixed up the dinner table. That night, Elizabeth took her usual seat close to Grace to have one hand available for Grace's chin so she didn't hit her face on the table. Gavin looked at Elizabeth with the most serious face and said, "Mom, it's OK, you can let her fall. We fixed the table—it's padded!" We all giggled a little and thanked Gavin for his help in protecting his sister. This will probably be a lot for him to live with, but because of it I believe he will be compassionate and thoughtful of the people around him.

Saying that Grace didn't sleep the best at night is an understatement. Grace normally woke up around 2:15 a.m. and got out of bed to go find us. She didn't know how to put her helmet on by herself, so she walked from her room to ours. Many times she didn't make it to our room before having a seizure, falling on the wood or tile floors. Most nights we woke to crying screams when she hit the floor. After a few nights of her hurting herself, we decided to put Grace in *our* bed for safety. The tile, granite, and hardwood floors we agonized over when building our house had become our greatest nightmare.

During the hospital stay when Grace started having her hallucinations, I decided to make a difficult phone call to my US National coach. She was at her worst and I couldn't *imagine* being away for so many weeks or months. I spoke with my Coach about my situation with Grace being in the hospital and not doing well. I told him I would have to step down. He came back and said he completely understood, that family came first, and told me if things were to get better he wanted me back with the squad in January. We had no way of knowing if Grace would get better, remain the same, or get worse. I told him thanks, but I didn't know if that would be happening.

When does a gold medal cost too much? It was a *hard*, and at the same time an *easy*, choice for me. I have my Gold Medals at home: Grace and Gavin. The price of the other Gold medal wouldn't have been worth it.

My two Gold Medals: Grace & Gavin

Gearing up for Ironman Wisconsin with my family.

Hiking the Napali Coast in Hawaii.

Hangin' "5" in Hawaii.

I ended up on a poster
with Lance
Armstrong!

Below: Team Glas
speaking engage-
ment showing
off my
"hardware."

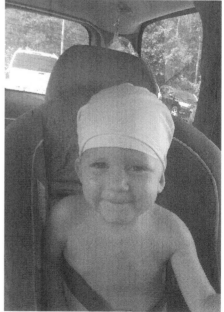

QUESTIONS ALWAYS ASKED

"Learn from yesterday, live for today, hope for tomorrow. The important thing is to not stop questioning."
−Albert Einstein

Below are several questions that I get asked at events, speeches, and in everyday life:

1.   How do you drive a car?

I am missing my right leg, so I have to cross my left leg over to the gas pedal and use my left leg to drive. I do have the option to use hand controls, or the choice of modifying my car to move the gas pedal over to the left side, but the cheapest and easiest option is to just drive with my left leg.

2.   How do you have sex?

Again, I am *only* missing my right leg.

3.   How was your relationship with your dad?

My relationship with my dad was good. However, we never really talked about the accident. It was always the *big white elephant* in the living room—always there, but never talked about. I know that he was proud of me. He told me before my first Ironman in Wisconsin that he knew that my life was full of challenges, but that I had done well for myself. That was all I needed. I never held him responsible or blamed him for the accident, and he knew that. Now, being a father myself, it has changed a lot for me. I can't imagine how he felt when the accident happened.

4.   Do people stare at you and does it bother you if they do?

People stare at me all of the time. I am different and don't try to hide it. I wear shorts whenever I can. People are intrigued when they see my prosthetic leg. It is only human nature to be curious about something different. I am guilty of it too. If I see someone with purple hair or a Mohawk, my eyes gravitate in that direction.

When I first lost my leg, I was very conscious when people stared at me. I really didn't like it. At times I even said something to them. Now, I am not bothered at all. Kids are the greatest when it comes to this. They have no barriers. They ask anything they think. At the pool, sometimes when I'm with the kiddos, other kids will stop in their tracks and come over and touch my leg. The funny part is that the parents are horrified, because of how they think I will feel. They fall over themselves to apologize for their child's comment. I make sure and say no problem at all and tell them that it is good to ask questions. I take time to explain to the kids about my accident and that I can do anything that they can, I just have to use a robot leg.

5.   Is your wife disabled?

My wife is not disabled. She has two legs!

6.   What will you do after sports?

I also believe opportunities will always show up when you need them. I will cross that bridge when the time comes. Sports will always be a big part of my life.

7.   Do you talk with returning Veterans?

I do talk with returning Veterans every chance I get. I have gone to Walter Reed to talk with some injured Vets and have introduced them to Wheelchair basketball. Most people think the hardest part about the injury is the missing leg. No, the *mental* side of the change is more life changing. These soldiers leave as big, strapping, proud men and women, ready to take on the world. They return missing body parts. They and society view them differently. They don't view themselves as whole people anymore. I am there to tell them that life will be different, but that they can still achieve anything they want. Some ask, "Will I still be OK with the girls now that I am an amputee?" My quick answer to them is to ask if they were popular with the girls before the accident. Nothing really changes unless you let it.

8.   What traits do you want to pass on to your children?

My work ethic. You don't have to be the smartest, most talented person in the world to be successful. If you have a strong work ethic you can always get to the top.

9.   You played wheelchair basketball in the NWBA (National Wheelchair Basketball Association). Wouldn't you rather play basketball in the NBA (National basketball Association)?

My answer to that is no! The only thing that would change is my bank account would have several more zeros after it. I am driven by life experiences, not money. My bank account is very *full* in that department. I am already gone away from my family enough. I can't imagine being gone from them even more with all of the games the NBA players play.

10.   What keeps you so positive?

I really believe that every day we wake up, we have a choice—is it going to be a good day or is it going to be a bad one? I try and make a good choice and choose a good day. Most of what happens to us can be handled in a positive way.

11.   Do you ever have bad days and how do you
        handle them?

I do have bad days. I try and limit them by thinking
about all of the great things I have going on in my life,
like my family. When I am really having a bad day, I
think of Grace and what she went through with her
seizures. Then it is really hard to have that bad of a
day.

12.   What is the worst part about being
        disabled?

Water! My Artificial legs are not waterproof, so I have
to take my leg off to swim. For me, the worst part about
being disabled is taking a shower away from my house.
Most showers, you have to step in to over a small lip
and close the door. As an amputee, I have to hop into
the shower. This is very dangerous when it is wet and
gets very slippery. Some of my amputee friends have
fallen and broken their good legs. I am very careful
while taking a shower. Also, water parks are very difficult. I have to hop up the steps to go down the water
slide.

13.   What is the best part of being disabled?

I get to board first on the airlines and it's better than a
fast pass at Disney. Membership—a Disability Card—has
it rewards. I board first to have room for my extra legs
I am bringing. If I board with everyone else, I can't find
enough space in the overhead bins.

14.   What do you want to achieve next?

I would love to someday climb Mount Everest. How cool would it be to really be on top of the World!

15.   Is your leg comfortable?

That is a loaded question. The leg itself is not the most comfortable. I would probably say the running leg is the least comfortable of all my legs. It is about like running on your knees. You can do it, but there is discomfort. However, without the leg, I couldn't run or be very active. So, I would rather have some discomfort.

My stump is very short below the knee—I only have five inches. They had to remove some of my back for the skin graft to save the knee. My stump is basically all fat and no muscle. I only have the tibia bone. This means my leg is a really hard fit for my prosthesis. When I run, I have to take my leg off about every two miles because all of the pistoning and friction that happens when I run. I have to sit down, take my liner off, clean off the sweat, and put then liner back on correctly. I lose a lot of time every two miles. But, I am not complaining, because I can still run and do some pretty amazing things.

16.   What is your favorite thing to do with your kids?

One of my favorite things is swimming at the pool with my two kiddos. They really enjoy swimming.

Swimming was one of the things we used to do when Grace was having so many seizures. It sounds strange that we would take our child that had seizures to the pool. But, for some reason, when she was around the water and in constant physical activity, she had fewer seizures – plus she LOVED it. Gavin has a natural talent for swimming and loves playing in the water. So, these are special times for us.

17. What did you do with your Paralympic Bronze Medal?

It's in a box in my exercise room. I haven't had it mounted for a couple of reasons. One reason is that I travel with it when I do speeches, because people like to see it. The other reason is that I always thought I would get a Gold Medal, and that I would rather have mounted. Maybe it's time to reconsider that.

18. Where do you get your legs made?

A company called ASTEP Ahead Prosthetics makes my legs. They are in Hicksville, New York. The legs are highly specialized. You can't buy them at Wal-Mart.

19. How long does it take to make the legs?

When I first lost my leg—over thirty years ago—it took at least a month to make one leg. At ASTEP Ahead Prosthetics, they can make an everyday walking leg, a running leg, and a cycling leg in about three days.

LESSONS LEARNED FROM MY GIFTS

When I do races, I have to tell you that I really enjoy passing someone with two legs. When a woman passes a male athlete in the triathlon world, that is known as "getting chicked." When I pass an athlete with two legs, I like to think to myself that they just "got cripped."

If I pass someone with two legs, it typically can have two different outcomes on that person. Many times, people are motivated and driven to push harder after they see me pass, and often say very positive things to me. Sometimes though, it has the opposite effect—the athlete I pass becomes depressed and defeated thinking that they are deficient somehow because they just got passed by a guy with one leg.

If I—or someone that makes you question your abilities—ever pass you, remember that success and hard work comes in all shapes and sizes. Thinking, "I just got passed by a guy with one leg" is not defeat. Instead, think about the victory. "I am so lucky that I have made this journey and I will get to the finish."

My life has, so far, been full of tragedy, joy, success, winning, finishing, loving, and fun. You will hear me say often that you need to recognize and embrace the gifts that are given to you each day. It's true. If you look back on tragedy or sadness, there is good that comes out of it, even if you can't see it then. Embrace that and know that you *will* see the victory.

Take my leg, for instance. Who in their right mind would view that as something good? I do. I never would have gotten to participate in world-renowned events like the Paralympics. I would have never met my wife and had my two beautiful children. I would have never made the great friends I have in my life because of where I lived and where I have traveled. I would have never gotten to travel to over forty-five countries doing things I love. I would have never tried an Ironman.

Also, take Grace—her condition is unbelievably frustrating and bad for her. No child should ever have to endure what she has gone through, but I know first-hand that she will be *stronger* for it. Our family will be stronger. Gavin will be protective and compassionate. We would have never known the wonderful people at Grace's school, Access Schools. We would have never known how to find humor in tragedy. Without the tragedy of her last hospital stay, where she almost died from the seizure drug reaction, we wouldn't be sitting here now, seizure free. We don't know why that happened, and sometimes we get too afraid to ask why. But *she is better.*

What about not finishing Ironman Kentucky? My whole life has been the successes I have made. However, this was *not* a success in my book, but I have learned more about myself from that experience than I could have imagined. I am human and I *will fail,* but that's OK. It's how you get back up and proceed from those failures that's the gift. I am stronger for having that experience. I am not going to lie and say I enjoyed it, but life is a series of victories and you have to work in between those victories to get to the next one. Most importantly, you have to be able to recognize when you have one.

Giving up the Gold Medal—this is probably the hardest one for me personally. However, I have amazing memories and time with my family. My daughter and son will know *they came first*. This frees up time for me to realize new goals and help others realize their dreams. I have realized it's not all about me all the time. It's my responsibility to help others recognize their victories and accomplishments. Besides, I have my Gold medals at home—what is better than that?

The passing of my father: My father was not a happy man most of the time, but he taught me how to embrace an experience and make it my own. Don't give up—it's not an option. After his passing, I have done a lot of reflecting on his influence in my life—good and bad. I wish we could have talked more about my accident, but that isn't an option now.

Don't ever live your life with regrets. Given my father's sudden passing, my accident, Grace's medical condition, and many other things, I am fully aware that life is short and you may not get that opportunity tomorrow to be happy. Choose to embrace your gifts now. Each day is a gift and you *have* to view it that way.

APPENDIX — "8-IN-8"

"To achieve the impossible;
it is precisely the unthinkable that must be thought."
–Tim Robbins

I think that most people want to be healthy and thin. However, nobody wants to diet or eat right. Most people want to live a long life, not too many want to exercise to make that happen. Everyone I know wants money, yet only a few work hard. Most successful people are in control of their feelings and form a habit of doing things that unsuccessful people really don't like to do. I believe the bookends of success are the *start* and the *finish*.

Every year I *celebrate* my anniversary of losing my leg. It might be a fun dinner out with my family or a purchase of something I have been wanting. But, on the thirtieth anniversary of losing my leg at the age of eight – it was time to do something big. Could I compete and finish eight Ironman distance triathlons in eight months? Decisions and confidence help us start and discipline helps us finish. This is why I love the Ironman so much and why I chose that venue to do this *celebration*. With my journey to complete the 8-in-8—as with starting most dreams, the hardest part was making the decision to start. Once I had come up with my goal, I was one hundred percent committed to it. When people start diets or paths to a healthy lifestyle, many times the hardest part is making that start.

The start of my Ironman dream of 8-in-8 was actually registering for each event. Each race was at least six hundred dollars, so I was all in at that point. The other end of success was the finish. In my journey, the finish line was truly the finish line of every race. Words can't explain the feeling of crossing each one of those finish lines. When I crossed each finish line, I knew I was a role model for my children and others. If they believed wholeheartedly in themselves, no matter what obstacles lay in front of them, they could accomplish their goals.

What helps each of us get to the finish line is discipline. Between the start and finish is the actual journey. I *really* love the journey. I had to wake up most mornings at 3 a.m. to get on the bike trainer to work out before my family woke up. This was *only* possible with discipline. If you find that discipline in yourself, the journey of the ups and downs becomes an amazing story and you will get to that finish line.

LESSON LEARNED AT IRONMAN ST. GEORGE
There are days you will have to rely on strangers.

I finally got approval and entry into each of the eight Ironman races at the last minute, so flights were an issue. My wife will tell you that I am not the best at detailed planning. Planning for eight Ironman races in eight months was a feat for me in and of itself! I arrived in Las Vegas and rented a car to drive the two hours to St. George, Utah. My thought process was that I would arrive two hours before race registration closed. Details—I failed to factor in the time change from Las Vegas to Utah. Now I only had an hour. I got registered ten minutes before they closed. In triathlons, you have a lot of equipment to bring: swim caps, goggles, bike helmet, sunglasses, nutrition, water, towels, tennis shoes, multiple outfits, etc. Being an amputee brings that equipment level up one hundred percent. In addition to all of the normal equipment needed, I had to keep track of three different legs, liners, and stump socks.

There are transition times in triathlons that are the times it takes you to transition between the sports—swim-bike-run. Transition one, or T1, is your time from swim exit to the time you get on the bike. Transition two, or T2, is the time you take from the bike exit until you start your run portion of the race. The transition times are included in your overall time.

People sometimes ask me if I get special help, because I am physically challenged. The answer to that is *yes and no.* We don't get help in the form of moving forward—like carrying me or skipping difficult parts in a race. We do get what I like to call *extra protection.* I am allowed what is called a handler. That person can be a person of my choosing or a recruited volunteer. The handler is allowed to come down to the swim exit and help coordinate the removal of my wet suit, and then the important part, *handing me my leg!*

Some handlers are better than others. For example, at the 2005 International Triathlon Union World Championships in

Hawaii, my handler—bless her heart—dropped my leg in the ocean. I had a hard time getting my leg on and off after that swim.

With Ironman St. George being last second for me, I didn't have the opportunity to bring a handler along. The morning of the race I recruited a volunteer. He told me he would meet me at the race start to take my artificial leg then walk it back to the swim exit. Twenty minutes before the race my new friend/handler was nowhere to be found. Five minutes to race start, still no handler. Panic mode officially set in. I glanced around the crowd and found what looked like a trusting face and asked an unusual favor—people always are a little shocked when I try to give them my legs. I explained that the person that was going to help me was nowhere to be found and that I needed him to take my leg and liner to the swim exit and wait for me to finish the swim. He assured me my leg would make it to the swim exit. I am a very trusting person so I hopped toward the water and hoped for the best.

The water was a very cold fifty-seven degrees. After the race, I heard that the officials had to remove almost one hundred racers from the water because of the cold. The cold can literally take your breath away. I couldn't feel my hands or my stump after about the first mile. I ended up finishing the swim in a little over one hour and twenty minutes. My leg, as promised, was waiting for me. I profusely thanked my new friend and was off to get my bike. It took the next thirty miles on the bike before I could feel my hands or stump.

The bike course was beautiful, but very hilly. On the bike, I rode up on a friend whom I raced alongside on the run at

Ironman Wisconsin the previous year. We chatted back and forth a bit as we leap frogged some of the hilly sections of the bike course. The bike portion of the race is always my favorite part, but it is still a big pain on my bottom side.

The run portion is always my *least* favorite segment. Running is especially hard on the body, and even more so for an amputee. The run in St. George was brutal. I managed to keep a pretty steady pace by walking up the extreme climbs. In triathlons, unlike most sports, the average athlete gets to race alongside professionals. The pros usually get a head start of about ten minutes, and usually finish about four hours ahead of me. In an Ironman we all start the journey together. At the start of the race, it feels like everyone is out for themselves—you get hit, swam over, and kicked in the water. The swim is a contact sport in the beginning. As the race moves on, it feels like everyone is cheering the next person on to get to that finish line. I believe everyone knows the commitment and sacrifice that went into getting to that finish line. I am very pleased to say I finished in the daylight—thirteen hours and fourteen minutes. After you get past a certain time of day in the race, they hand out glow sticks, so you can see the athletes better after dark. A goal of mine is not to be handed a glow stick, although that has not always been the case for me.

LESSON LEARNED AT IRONMAN COEUR D'ALENE
Whenever you fall down, dust yourself off and get back on track.

My second Ironman race for the 8-in-8 journey was Ironman Coeur d'Alene in Idaho. This was my first time in that area. I brought my own handler with me this time—my favorite and most trusted handler, my beautiful wife, Elizabeth. She is a veteran and a real problem solver. We went through the game plan together to get the best result in transition. My three big requests were to hand me my leg, my Garmin Heart rate monitor, and to find a big strong guy for a stripper—not what you are thinking! The *stripper* is a person or people that help athletes rip off their wetsuits quickly.

My wife came through big time with the stripper. She found a big strong dude—so strong that while stripping my wetsuit off he pulled me off the chair I was sitting on and onto the beach. Now, I was sitting on the sandy beach all covered in sticky sand. This is an amputee's worst nightmare. I wiped off the best I could with the towel I had and moved through transition.

About three miles into the run, I noticed that I didn't have my Garmin Heart rate monitor on my wrist. Somehow in the transition, I failed to get the Garmin off of Elizabeth's wrist and onto mine. On the bike I didn't know how fast I was going or how hard my heart was working. The thing with Ironman racing, nothing usually goes as planned, so you have to deal the challenges and move forward. Problem solving is a necessary skill in triathlon.

About fifteen miles into the bike, my stump started hurting. The sand on my stump was acting like sand paper with my liner moving up and down. At the end of the one hundred and twelve mile bike ride, my stump was raw and tender. My wife met me again at the transition area and handed me my leg and my Garmin. She smiled and said. "Oops!" The run was very painful with the raw stump, but I managed to finish the race in thirteen hours and four minutes.

LESSON LEARNED AT IRONMAN LAKE PLACID
Take time to live in the moment!

The week prior to Ironman Lake Placid, my third of eight races, we went to Jamaica for my youngest sister's wedding. The food and drink at the all-inclusive resort was probably not the best for any of us, especially if you were trying to manage your weight. The food was also much different than what I was used to and so my diet was less than stellar that week. Then, add an open bar with not much else to do.

My sister's wedding was great. I believe it was everything they wanted it to be! After the ceremony we boarded a bus for a little adventure around the island for some cool photos and fun. Our first trip was Jimmy Buffet's Margaritaville. Everyone had a very stiff Margarita, then we were off to the next place. We boarded the bus and handed out the Red Stripe. The next stop was a little bar and restaurant that overlooked the ocean. We were told of caves and cliffs. We saw some people jumping off the cliffs and decided that that might be fun. Off we went, one by one, jumping into the ocean from a twenty-foot cliff. I jumped in foot first—like a tooth pick. Sometimes, I forget that I am an amputee. I don't know if that is a good thing or bad thing, but in this case it happened to be a bad thing. I jumped in, hit the water, and instantly bruised my stump. The end of my stump is very sensitive and very fragile. Like I tell my son sometimes, this was "not a good choice." The damage was done, so I went ahead and made a couple more jumps.

Our next stop was the world famous—or most dangerous bar in the world—Ricks Bar. It faces the ocean and has some pretty amazing views. They also have cliffs to jump from. The bar was packed with people watching a few people making the jump. The smallest cliff to jump from was twenty-five feet and the higher cliff was thirty-five feet. I decided before stepping into the place that I *was* going to jump. Sometimes just making that decision is the hardest part—to jump or not to jump.

I quickly made my way over to the cliff and sat down to remove my leg. I sent my wife down the steps to the water with my artificial leg so I would have it when I got out of the water. I had a better game plan for this higher jump. I was going to protect "Stumpy". I decided to tuck Stumpy behind my other knee to protect it from the water entry. I hopped my way up to the higher jump and jumped. It was an amazing adrenaline rush! I loved it and had no further damage to Stumpy. The crowd cheered like crazy.

Leaving Jamaica, I was ten pounds heavier and had a badly bruised stump. This is not exactly how you want the lead-up to go into your third Ironman in three months.

With my late notice of me doing my eight Ironman races, I was behind trying to find a reasonable hotel. With a lot of research I still couldn't come up with a place to stay for under three hundred and fifty dollars a night.

I finally got a call from a buddy saying I could stay with them in a rented farmhouse. I flew to Albany, New York, rented a car, and drove two and a half hours to Lake Placid. The place was beautiful—a lot of trees, mountains, and water. Race morning they were forecasting a lot of rain. As an amputee, rain is a big deal. We have to have a dry liner for maximum comfort. If the liner gets wet then it starts to slide and piston, leaving a lot of skin issues and painful bleeding.

When the race cannon fired, we still had no rain. I was super excited about that. The swim was beautiful, with the mountains in the background. I seeded myself in the middle of the pack, hoping to not get beat up. The swim is always a contact sport, but this one was brutal. The first lap everyone fought for their spot in the water. The first turn around I managed a good turn and remained out of a lot of contact. After the first loop of the swim, we had to get out of the water and go across a timing mat, then re-enter the water to start the second loop. When I exit the water, I have to crawl around the beach until I reach the timing mat and crawl to re-enter the second loop. I managed only to get in the way of a *couple* of people and only got knocked over a handful of times.

I got out of the water in one hour twelve minutes. The transition went pretty smoothly. I got out of my wetsuit and put on my leg with no problem. The bike part of the race had a lot of climbing and descents. The rain came out to play and made the first loop a bit on the dangerous side of things. On my way down the first descent, another rider crashed his bike in front of me, so I slowed down a lot—No need to take any chances for a few seconds gain. The last twenty miles of the first loop was full of hills. The second lap was much easier, because the roads were now dry.

The bike is always fun because you get to meet so many interesting people from all over the place. On this bike ride,

I managed to get a product sponsor from Infinit Nutrition. Speaking of nutrition, my stomach started to feel really yucky on about mile ninety of the bike. That wasn't a good sign of things to come. In an Ironman, if you don't stay on top of your nutrition, you run into trouble fast.

I went into T2 feeling OK. I quickly dismounted the bike, removed my bike leg from the bike, and clicked into my running leg, and then I was off to the changing tent. I removed all of the bike clothes and changed into my running clothes. I removed my bike leg liner and put on my running leg liner. The first couple of miles of the run are in town with a lot of crowd support. I felt fine those first few miles.

Around mile fourteen of the run, things started to take a turn for the worse. My stomach was still a mess. I was unable to eat much of anything after mile ninety of the bike. I started throwing up—dry heaving—which was not fun, especially knowing I still had 12.2 miles left. I knew I would finish, because I still had a lot of time remaining before the seventeen-hour cutoff, plus the fact that I am mentally strong and not a quitter.

The next six miles were very painful with a lot of stops for walking, puking, and to change my leg. Running for me is more difficult than the average amputee. My stump is very flabby with not a lot of muscle or padding. I also only have the tibia bone in my stump. My stump doesn't provide for the greatest fit. Simply put, I have to stop about every one and a half miles to check and re-adjust my liner. This task usually takes about sixty to ninety seconds from start to finish. I have to remove my liner, dry it off, check for any signs of wear, add or remove any stump socks depending on swelling, and repeat the process in reverse order to put my leg back on.

Around mile twenty of the run, my liner ripped. Going into the race, my liner had some wear, but I was sure I could at least get another race out of it. Leg liners—like most adaptive equipment—are very expensive. The liner cost around two thousand dollars each, so I try and get as many miles as I can out of them. It turned out to be a painful decision.

The liner provides an airtight surrounding for my stump. It has a pin at the end of the liner to hold my leg and liner together. With my liner ripped, it made for the most uncomfortable run possible.

Two things kept me going. First and foremost, I had never dropped out of a race—knock on wood. The second, I wore race number 179. This number is important in Ironman races, because of a young man who died of ALS—amyotrophic lateral sclerosis, or Lou Gehrig's disease. He suffered from the disease but was driven to complete the Ford Ironman World Championships in Kona, Hawaii. He finished the Ironman and literally *rolled* across the finish line. Now, those who wear that number always roll across the finish line to celebrate the life of that Warrior's Challenge. I knew no matter how much it hurt and no matter how bloody my stump got, I *would* make it to the finish line.

Three miles left in the race took us through the city of Lake Placid. I remember the people cheering. Crowd support and cheering is exactly what you need when you are feeling a lot of pain and completely wiped out. At that point, I could hear the announcer Mike Riley yell out, "You are an Ironman!" I was not to be stopped. I wanted him to yell that out for me. I gritted my teeth and pressed forward. At the finish line, thankfully, I remembered to pay my respects to Blazeman, and rolled across the finish line to honor him. I held up three fingers to signify my third Ironman in three months.

My friend who also completed the Ironman met me at the finish line. Upon seeing my friend, I almost collapsed and told him I needed to go to the medical tent. Thankfully, he was a *big* friend. He picked me up and took me to the medical tent. At the medical tent, they weighed me, and I had lost 12 pounds—they weigh you when you check in and use this to determine how much liquid you lost during the race. I was given two bags of IVs and my open wounds on my stump were treated. I still finished the race in thirteen hours and fifty-five minutes.

LESSON LEARNED AT IRONMAN LOUISVILLE, KY
You already know about this one! Let's move on...

LESSON LEARNED AT IRONMAN WISCONSIN
Always believe in your dreams. Never let anyone place limits on you.

Usually, two nights before an Ironman, there is always an athlete banquet and athlete briefing to get all of the athletes motivated and informed. Ironman Wisconsin, I was chosen to be the Ford Everyday Hero. They came to my sister's house to film me riding, running, and to do a brief interview. More importantly, the winner of this award got a *free* spot into any Ironman race in North American, except Kona. I was guaranteed to do at least one Ironman next year.

Four hours before the banquet, I received a phone call from the voice of Ironman—Mike Riley. He congratulated me on the award, told me he had seen the great video they did of me, and that he had an idea for the banquet to change it up. He wanted to know if I would introduce him for the banquet. Are you kidding me? Normally Mike Riley stands near the front and one of the producers announces him. I am never one to turn down an honor like that, so I said yes to the plan. He sat with my family before the banquet started. Then I had the honor of introducing him. Mike Riley is the Ironman icon who says at the finish line, "Jeff Glasbrenner, you are an Ironman!" It was such an honor and definitely a cool experience for me. At the end of the banquet, Ironman presented me with the Ford Everyday Hero Award. They showed a pretty amazing four-minute video of me that showed my story. At the end of that video, I got to say a few words to the three thousand plus crowd. Surreal, to say the least.

All of the Ironman races are a bit different in how things are set up and how the transition area is arranged. Normally, your bags with equipment/clothes are kept in an area in front of the change tent. You simply yell out your number and go to the row where your bags are stored. The Ironman races allow Physically Challenged athletes to have a fixed area so we can store our adaptive equipment.

The transition area at Ironman Wisconsin is a large building called the Monona Terrace. I placed my equipment in the men's changing tent and labeled it PC. My sister was my handler for this race. She followed me to the transition area. I set up all of my gear in my area. Then, we decided we could use the restroom before going toward the swim start. I always have a couple of last minute nervous pees.

Both the men's and women's lines were very long, full of athletes with the same idea we had. I told her I would meet her outside of the women's line, because her line was longer. I waited my line out and exited the restroom and waited. I paced back and forth for another few minutes, looking for her in the crowd. Still no luck, and time was running out. I decided to wade through the crowd down to the swim start. I made it close to the swim start and was starting to get nervous—not for my race start, but for my sister and her task of protecting my leg and meeting me at the swim exit.

My sister is a very resourceful person. She found me with eight minutes to spare. She quickly helped me zip up my wetsuit and took my leg and liner. She gave me a quick hug and wished me luck. I crawled a couple hundred feet with the mass of athletes waiting to get into the water. With two minutes to start, I was at the water. The cannon went off and the confusion started.

The first ten minutes of the swim are important. This is the time when a lot of important energy can be wasted. Athletes tend to be very aggressive at the start. Many times, athletes go too hard at the race start and fade quickly. I'd done this many times, so I conserved my energy and tried to stay away from overly aggressive arms and legs. The plan worked and I made it to the first turn around feeling pretty good.

The turns are usually very difficult. Everyone tends to bunch up and it slows down lots. This is the time that you usually get kicked in the face or the groin. I did some defensive swimming—guarding the important areas with a wax on, wax off approach. I completed the first of two laps without incident. The second lap I found some quick feet to follow. In the swim, if you can get behind another swimmer's feet, you can draft and expend less energy. The second lap was even faster and I saved more energy.

I exited the water in one hour and nine minutes and hopped over to my sister. She helped me out of my wetsuit and handed me my equipment. The run from the swim to the transition area is a very unique experience at Ironman Wisconsin. You actually have to run up a helix. The helix is a paved spiral road up the side of the parking lot. My sister and I ran up the helix with thousands of spectators cheering us on. Half way up the helix, my sister asked me how I was doing, I told her the swim was great. About thirty seconds later, my sister turned to me and said while running, "If you do the race again next year, I will too!" I was really motivated now to show her how cool this race/journey really is!

I went into the men's change tent and my sister waited outside ready to help me once I got to my bike. I did a quick change and we were off running to my bike. We arrived at my bike, pulled the bike from the rack, and I ran with it to the bike mount line. I pushed the button to release my running leg and stepped into my cycling leg. I was now all set for the one hundred and twelve mile bike ride. The only misstep that happened was I somehow lost my heart rate monitor—HRM—strap in the swim or on that long helix run. I usually train with the HRM to gauge my work effort. The HRM acts like a RPM gauge in a car—it measures the workload. In a race that long it is always a good idea to keep a close eye on how the body is working and responding.

The bike course in Wisconsin is one of the harder bike segments in the Ironman circuit. It has a lot of hills. This race always has a lot of crowd support on the whole course, plus it was my home state, which meant my entire family could be there. On three of the bigger climbs, the crowd support rivals that of the Tour De France with the fans only leaving a few feet path for the riders to go over the hill. I learned my lesson from years past not to get caught up in the adrenaline rush from all of those people cheering you on and kept an even pace. The bike course is an out and back with two loops in the middle, so you get the repeat the hilly section twice. I finished the bike in six hours and eighteen minutes. I got off the bike and my sister was waiting for me with my leg and a lot of encouragement. I made a quick transition and was set for the 26.2 mile run.

It was a rough couple of weeks leading up to this race. I DNF'd my first race at Ironman Louisville late into the run. My Dad passed away in a farming accident. However, Ironman Wisconsin was my favorite Ironman by far. I have had the honor of racing the Ironman World Championships in Kona twice, but Wisconsin stills wins out.

First off, it was where I was born and raised. The run course at Ironman Wisconsin is really personal and emotional for me. About halfway through the first lap, the run course takes the athletes parallel to the University of Wisconsin Hospital. This was the same hospital where I spent forty-seven days fighting for my life That same hospital was where the doctors told me I could no longer participate in any sport what so ever for fear of hurting myself or others. I ran by that hospital—the very place where I thought my dreams had died—and thought to myself, *I did it. Not only am I doing sports, I am doing what is considered the most grueling one-day sporting event in the world.*

I really don't like when people place limits on you, and I really dislike when individuals place limits on themselves. If they really want to accomplish something, work hard to make it happen! That being said, the best part of that day was the finish line. I had a predetermined time that I wanted to finish the race. If I finished in that time, my kiddos would still be awake and there to share that moment with me. So with that carrot in front of me, I am happy to say I got to share that with them.

LESSON LEARNED AT IRONMAN FLORIDA
Surround yourself with people who believe in you!

Ironman Florida was my sixth Ironman that year. It was the first of three for the month of November. I woke up at 1 a.m. on November fourth and drove the eleven hours from Little Rock to Panama City to get to the registration on time. It was very cold and windy, so I decided to try out my disc wheel to see if it would be OK with the high winds. I was about forty-five minutes into the test ride and I had a flat tire on my disc wheel. My mind was made up to use my regular rear wheel with spokes. It was a stroke of good/bad luck! It was much better to have a flat on a practice ride than during the race. The bad luck part of it was that I had to walk almost a mile back to the hotel in my cycling leg. That leg is not meant for walking.

The swim: It was as forecasted a very cold morning for Florida's standard—thirty-eight degrees. The swim start for Ironman Florida is a mass beach start. It was at low tide, so there was quite a long hop/crawl to get to where you could finally swim. In the water, it was the usual washing machine swim until we made the first turn around, then it thinned out nicely.

Florida is a two-loop course making you exit the water on your first lap going over a timing mat on the beach. I again had to crawl in the shallow water and exit for the first lap then go around the timing map and start my second loop. It was pretty cool to have everyone at the turn around give an extra cheer as I crawled around the timing mat. The second lap was much less crowded and I made my way back to the swim exit with ease. My handler—my sister—was waiting as promised on the right side of the exit.

I finished the swim in one hour and nine minutes. My transition was very smooth. I got my bike clothes and equipment on pretty fast, considering how crowded it was in the transition area. I then met my sister outside the change tent and we ran to my bike. I was off for the bike one hundred and twelve miles. My T1 time was seven minutes—not bad considering all of the equipment and leg changes!

The bike was very cold and windy. The wind felt like it was always in my face, even when we turned directions. I felt really good on the bike and made sure to be very diligent on taking my Infinit nutrition every fifteen minutes, along with water. I made it to the turnaround still feeling really good. I grabbed my special needs bag with my other Infinit bottle and continued on my way. I got off the bike feeling pretty good, especially in the stomach department. My bike time was five hours and forty-six minutes—19.4 average MPH). My sister was waiting on the right hand side of the dismount area and she handed me my running leg. I made it in and out of the transition area in seven minutes.

The run: Starting the run not completely destroyed and without stomach problems is a great feeling. I took it pretty easy for the first three miles to get my running legs. My wife, coach, and sister were at key points along the race to cheer me on. It was a two loop run course that was extremely flat. The weather didn't warm up much, making it a relatively cold day.

My marathon run time was four hours and forty minutes. As always. it was an amazing feeling crossing the finish line. My finish time was eleven hours and forty-nine minutes my fastest time so far that year.

LESSON LEARNED AT IRONMAN ARIZONA
Have a plan and stick to it!

Ironman Arizona was only two weeks after Ironman Florida. To say I was rested and recovered would be a *big* stretch. After some recovery workouts, I was as ready as I could be to take on Ironman number seven. My awesome host and friend, Gary, picked me up at the airport and gave me the weather forecast for race day. He said it was going to be in the sixties with forty percent chance of rain. However, he was quick to add that the weatherman never got it right and that it only rains about thirteen days out of the year in Phoenix.

The swim: They just recently filled the Tempe Town Lake because the dam broke months prior to the race. They must have filled it with ice water. I got in the water five minutes to race start. The water was really cold, but when that cannon went off, it was survival of the fastest. There were two thousand five hundred racers and twelve hundred first timers, so as usual it was a pretty physical swim for the first half-mile. After that everything seemed to thin out and I got into a good groove. I exited the water in one hour seven minutes and crawled across the timing mat to meet Gary holding my running leg.

I ran to the change tent. I did a quick job of changing into everything and raced to my bike. I quickly grabbed my bike from the rack and started running out to the bike start line. I went to step into my cycling leg already on my bike and realized why my T1 time was so fast...I had forgotten my sock for my good foot. I am a person for not looking back, so I threw Gary my running leg and said, I will see you in about 6 hours. My T1 time was four minutes.

The bike: The bike course for Ironman Arizona is not the most challenging course on the Ironman circuit. So, even without a sock, I was still hoping for a fast day, but it was very windy. We had twenty-five to thirty mile per hour winds. The course is a three-loop course so we get to experience the winds in every direction. One section of the course is about an eight-mile section where you have a two to three percent grade up, but then you get to go down it. On the uphill section, we had the wind to our back. The down section we had the wind in our faces. It was difficult to get a lot of speed in either direction.

On the second loop it started to rain. This made things a bit slippery and I saw a few bikes go down. The third loop, it rained again. The wind stayed constant the whole time. I was very lucky I didn't get any blisters on my wet, sockless foot. I finished the bike in six hours and five minutes—almost 18.5 mph.

The run: The run course is also a three loop course. About one mile into the run, Chrissie Wellington—on her way to an Ironman Marathon record—tapped me on the back and said, "Way to go!" as she zoomed going by. I was happy and disappointed at the same time. She was on lap three and I was just starting...then I remembered the pros had a ten-minute head start and laughed. The first loop I was feeling really good. I executed a great Infinit nutrition plan on my bike and my stomach was feeling great. I normally have to stop and adjust my artificial leg every mile and a half to clear the sweat away and to make sure everything was OK with my stump. On the second lap, my leg was starting to go numb. It was rubbing on a nerve or something and putting my leg asleep.

On the third lap, I had to stop every half a mile to deal with the numb stump. I didn't want to push it too hard, because I had my final Ironman in seven days—Ironman Cozumel. It started to rain again on the third lap. I finished Ironman Arizona in twelve hours and nineteen minutes. A quick trip back to Little Rock, then off to Mexico for Ironman Cozumel.

LESSON LEARNED AT IRONMAN COZUMEL
You are much stronger than you ever thought possible.

Getting to the finish line makes for big smiles.

This was my eighth Ironman in eight months—the race I was looking most forward too! It was my third full Ironman Race this month. I recover fairly fast, but this was pushing it. At the final race of my journey, my mother was up to the task of being my handler. She thought this journey was really crazy, but supported and believed in me one hundred percent.

The swim: The swim takes place at Chankanaab Park—a local attraction where you can swim with the dolphins. This was only my second Ironman without the use of the wetsuit. I was told by the locals that there can be a heavy current at times, then again it could also be very calm, all on the same day. When the cannon went off I found myself near the front middle. That was the first Ironman that I never got beat up. From the start, everyone seemed to be playing nice. I made it to the first turnaround with no heavy contact. I made it to the second turnaround and felt fine.

Exiting the water was my only challenge. There were a series of steps that took you up to the pier. However, the first step didn't start until you were on top of the water. I had to reach the back of the steps and pull myself up with my arms. I found my mom nervously waiting for me at the top of the steps. She handed me a towel, my leg liner, and my running leg. I exited the water at one hour and five and crossed the timing mat at one hour and nine minutes. I ran the long distance to the T1 area and changed into my bike kit.

I ran the maze where the bikes were placed and grabbed my awesome Orbea Ordu. My mom was nowhere to be seen to hand off my running leg, so I quickly asked a random gentleman if he would hang onto my leg until my mother showed up. He quickly took my leg and held it in the air and yelled, "Awesome!" It's always a surprise to people when I throw them my leg. I made it out of T1 in less than five minutes.

The bike: The weather had already started to warm up. I was expecting to have a lot of wind on the bike. The first loop of three started out great with no wind. I was averaging about twenty-one miles per hour for the first loop. I started the second loop and it really started getting windy. My speed dropped to seventeen and a half miles per hour. The third loop was more of the same with the wind and heat. The bike course was beautiful along the ocean, filled with a lot of spectators. I made it to T2 in six hours and fifteen minutes. I quickly found my mother, who was guarding my running leg. I took off my cycling leg and handed it to her and she gave me my running leg. I got in and out of T2 in less than five minutes.

The run: The run started out very hot and windy. It felt like we had no protection from the sun. However, the great part of the run was that it was full of spectators. They were amazing. The hardest part for me on the run—other that the fact that my legs were not exactly rested from Ironman Arizona—was that the first three miles of the run loop had stamped concrete birds into the road. This made it much more difficult for me to run because of the uneven surfaces, so I jammed my knee several times.

With the excessive heat, I was forced to dump water and ice on my head and body. This is a good move to lower my core temperature, but the water found its way to my leg liner. On the second loop of the three-loop course, the sun let up. I had to continue to stop and make adjustments to my liner because of the heat. I finished the run in six hours and seven minutes. I finished the race in a much slower time than I wanted—thirteen hours and forty-four minutes. However, it was the most amazing feeling to cross that finish line at my eighth Ironman that year.

LESSON LEARNED AT IRONMAN DISTANCE LITTLE ROCK
(to make up for not finishing Ironman Louisville)

Everything happens for a reason!

I spent the week leading up to my Little Rock Ironman distance race in Breckenridge, Colorado for the Hartford Ski Spectator. I was there doing a couple of speeches for Hartford clients. We skied all week. It was a nice way to get in some training at altitude though.

This last Ironman was not an Ironman branded event. It was my make-up Ironman to replace my DNF in Louisville. My friends and a few supporters put the race on for me. In distance it was the same— a 2.4 mile swim, a one hundred and twelve mile bike, and a 26.2 mile run. The race took place in my hometown of Little Rock. The swim was at the Little Rock Athletic Club, my home base for most of my Ironman and wheelchair basketball training.

I did eighty-eight laps in the fifty-yard pool. A few people swam the race with me, showing support along the way. I got out of the pool in one hour and five minutes. I made my T1 area in the men's restroom. The weather on this day in Little Rock was thirty-five degrees with a lot of wind. I made sure to really layer my clothing and mentally prepare for a long, cold day. I wouldn't have to worry about overheating like the Ironman Louisville event.

The bike section started out with a hill and a lot of car traffic. My coach rode along with me on the course. Another friend took my truck as the aid vehicle to help with the traffic and carry extra water and nutrition. She was awesome, always providing motivation and a smile. My coach made sure never to let me draft, only keeping me company and keeping me on task.

About sixty miles into the one hundred and twelve mile ride, I came across an old abandoned farm. On this farm, I saw a junked out John Deere Tractor. It was the same model John Deere 60 that I lost my leg on. I thought to myself, *How fitting. This is why I took on this challenge, because of being on that tractor at the wrong time.* Now, passing by that tractor really gave me strength. It was like reliving that tragic moment, but also knowing that I had the strength to keep going in any direction that I wanted. This time it was a finish line in Little Rock.

The rest of the ride was very flat in terrain, but very windy, so it took a lot out of my legs. Finishing the one hundred and twelve mile ride was an awesome feeling. T2 area was at Orbea's USA headquarters in North Little Rock. This company believed in me and my journey. I ride their awesome bike. They let me use their building for my own personal T2 area. I got my running leg and other running items and made the change.

A few friends and supporters were they to send me off running. I also had a few runners who ran with me. That was awesome and made the journey much more enjoyable. The course zigzagged through North Little Rock and Little Rock. The last part of the marathon followed much of the Little Rock Marathon course. Nearing the end of the marathon portion, I had about fifteen runners with me, which was an amazing experience.

A couple of days before my last race in Little Rock, I did a TV interview with my friend and fellow triathlete, Kevin Kelly, from Fox 16, a local affiliate. The news segment was great, telling my story and my long journey. It was a big finish for me, because a lot of people heard about it from the news story and showed up to watch me finish.

A local race organizer—DLT Events—came to Little Rock and put up a finishing chute. They had live music and announced me as an Ironman distance finisher. They even made me a Little Rock Medal—it was *actually* a little rock. The race finish was a the Capitol building in Little Rock in a small park called Victory Park. This was the most amazing feeling. It was the end of an incredible journey.

Looking back, having the experience in Little Rock would not have been possible if I had finished Ironman Louisville. It's funny how things work out.

As I have experienced my various gifts throughout my life, I am beginning to realize that it is equally as important to help other people recognize their gifts and dreams. One such dream that has been realized is that of my friend Dr. Rob Lyle.

Just before we entered the hospital the last time with Grace (when she was having her hallucinations), I had gone to a local triathlon just hours before our unplanned trip to the emergency room. At the Triathlon, I became reacquainted with Rob, whom I had met at Ironman Louisville. Neither of us finished Ironman Louisville. He had signed up for five Ironman races and had never officially finished one.

We talked a lot after we successfully finished the local Olympic distance triathlon. He told me that he was going to race at Ironman Arizona and that he was worried about it, and that he really wanted to become an Ironman finisher. I loved seeing how passionate he was about this Ironman journey.

When we were admitted to the hospital, I was desperate for people with knowledge around us to help us with Grace's situation. I reached out to him. He was awesome and was patient in answering any and all questions we had. It was great learning more about him and what he did as a doctor. He spent most of his life helping others live theirs. He and the other doctors we met really care for Grace. They went above and beyond just being doctors. They put the human side back in medicine. Those doctors are a true inspiration to me.

It occurred to me that it would be awesome to give something back to someone that has saved so many lives and helped so many more overcome an accident or illness. I told him that I would help him become an Ironman finisher; race with him, mentor him and be there every step of the way. He immediately accepted. He asked what I wanted in return. I told him a thank you at the finish line.

Letter from Rob:

To know Jeff Glasbrenner is to know a man of contagious extremes. I had my first heart-to-heart discussion with the world champion Paralympian and Ironman triathlete after a local triathlon race where I had suffered a major setback. Thinking I was on track in my training to tackle, yet again, my goal of completing an Ironman, I had struggled mightily in this local race and sat dejected at the post race celebrations. I had struggled for some time with an old knee injury and I feared the odds were just too great to successfully finish an Ironman race of 140.6 miles. However, I soon found a new enthusiastic friend with an upbeat and positive outlook that sought to help me find the positives in an otherwise negative experience.

Where I felt despair and saw futility, Jeff saw opportunity. Knowing of my plans for Ironman Arizona in three months, he emailed me the next day with an extraordinary offer—he would get a slot for the race and go with me to help make sure I completed my goal!

I was astounded that this man would sacrifice his time and expenses to support me. I was more amazed that he was actually able to gain entry, as the race was long since closed. Yet, like so many of his efforts, failure in getting this opportunity was not an option. Over the few remaining months prior to the race, we trained together and I would soon gain the confidence that this dream was in fact possible.

Race day approached and—like my failed effort at Ironman Louisville the year before—I approached with an expected trepidation.

However, unlike Louisville, I was better prepared and had gained a quiet confidence from the skills learned from Jeff, and knowing I would not be alone in this journey. I had panicked at Louisville not long after entering the Ohio River and had been forced to stop at many of the kayakers to regain my composure. In the hysteria and disorganization of my swim, I had cramped up and had barely been able to finish the swim in an official time - only *to later drop out mid-way through the bike. I may have had more confidence going into Arizona, but I still feared jumping into that water—it was sixty-one degrees.*

Most, if not all, of the Ironman swims are chaotic, as several thousand triathletes battle for position in a churning mass of water. The swim is the most stressful of the Ironman events as evidenced by a number of recent deaths from healthy athletes. This knowledge weighed heavily on me as I prepared to jump into Tempe Town Lake with Jeff. But Jeff had a plan to briefly delay our entry to avoid the masses and better get our bearings for a swim that could take me close to two hours. What I did not know is that he would chart our course and seek to actively protect me from those who wandered into my path. I eventually found a rhythm and was able to make good progress as we made our turn for the swim finish. With Jeff running interference and pushing our pace, I exited the water in an amazing time of one hour and thirty-nine minutes. I made my way to the first transition while Jeff hustled us to get warm, get changed, and get out on the bike.

Leaving that first transition is still an amazing memory, as my greatest fear had been the swim. Having overcome my greatest challenge and my greatest fears, this bike ride was going to be a piece of cake, right?

The bike course at Ironman Arizona is a three-loop course that I remember thinking was mostly flat terrain. However, the miles just did not seem to pass, and the wind and fatigue certainly made what little elevation present seem like a Category One climb as my legs felt dead on that first loop. Yet, I knew I had to keep Jeff in my sights, as our plan had been for him to set a pace that would keep me on track to finish the race in under seventeen hours. I struggled to get into a rhythm and never felt comfortable, finishing loop one at a pace much slower than planned. Jeff then pushed the pace and I immediately became angered by his insensitivity to my plight. For a time I really struggled, but somehow through this anger, I managed to pick up the pace and negatively split the third loop with an overall time and pace exactly in keeping with Jeff's plan for the race—the dream was still alive. Jeff's psychological maneuver had helped me push through the pain and fatigue, helping me avoid the disastrous DNF as I had experienced at Louisville.

Now came the hard part—the marathon. I had successfully run a number of marathons over the years and had nearly eclipsed the sub-four hour mark in my best effort at Chicago in 2002. However, now because of severe degenerative osteoarthritis in my left knee, I had done little run training for this marathon and merely hoped I could walk/run the last 26.2 miles in under eight hours. It would be a major struggle for Jeff as well, as his typical marathon times were much faster, meaning he would have to devise a walk/run strategy for his prosthesis, and deal with the potential wear and tear the additional time would have on his stump.

We began the marathon with an unusual amount of energy and vigor and actually ran a lot more than I expected. I remember having a delusion, thinking we might actually be able to run this in six hours—but then the wheels began to come off. I began having a stabbing pain in my medial knee and was forced to stop multiple times. I would later learn Jeff was struggling with a lot of pain in his stump as well, but he never let me know. He continued to push and encourage me while insisting that we were going to make it—and we soldiered on, step by step, through an enveloping darkness as the minutes ticked by. I found myself mentally incapable of calculating our pace, and remember just wanting to lie down and get off my knee, but Jeff knew where we had to be and kept us on track. Soon we saw and heard those sights and sounds that could only mean the finish was near.

*I am sure Mike Reilly said, "Rob Lyle, **you** are an Ironman," but it never registered, because on that night I crossed that finish line eternally grateful to be arm-in-arm with a man who laid it on the line to help me realize a lifelong dream, a man who long ago turned tragedy into opportunity, and today turned dreams into reality. For the honor and privilege of this incredible journey, Jeff Glasbrenner, I thank you.*